Advance Praise

Reading this book feels like your best girlfriend (who also happens to be an expert stylist) is sitting across the table teaching you everything you never knew you needed to know about expressing yourself through fashion, as a woman and a #ladyboss

- Melinda Parrish
Plus-size Supermodel

Smart, practical, thoughtful, original. Rachel Nachmias has fit the proverbial nail on the head with her insights and analysis. This book was like getting a lightening blast of energy and hope rolled into one bolt! Equally inspirational and practical. I can do this!

- Tracy Themes
Financial Advisor, TracyTheemes.com

Rachel's approach lets women master shopping, find peace, and love themselves all over again. Whether appearing on film or simply getting dressed every day, your appearance will be more beautifully you than ever before. *The Face of the Business* is filled with strategies to help you do this for yourself. Along with the most relevant insights on the meaning of presentation for today's woman, you'll find page after page of practical, do-able advice. Today can be the day to believe that you're ready to play the lead role in your videos and your life.

- Christine Scaman
founder of 12 Bluep

T0163756

Presenting yourself well on camera can drive dramatic upswing in your business. This book offers tips, tactics and approaches for dressing to appear on camera, which makes it easy to create videos both you and your audience love.

- Lee Heyward

Image Strategist and author of *Strategically Suited*

the **FACE** of the BUSINESS

the *face* of the BUSINESS

*Develop Your Signature Style,
Step Out from Behind the Curtain
& Catapult Your Business on Video*

RACHEL NACHMIAS

NEW YORK

NASHVILLE • MELBOURNE • VANCOUVER

The Face of the Business

Develop Your Signature Style, Step Out from Behind the Curtain and Catapult Your Business on Video

Published in New York, New York, by Morgan James Publishing in partnership with Difference Press. Morgan James is a trademark of Morgan James, LLC. www.MorganJamesPublishing.com

The Morgan James Speakers Group can bring authors to your live event. For more information or to book an event visit The Morgan James Speakers Group at www.TheMorganJamesSpeakersGroup.com.

ISBN 9781683505235 paperback
ISBN 9781683505242 eBook
Library of Congress Control Number: 2017905324

Cover Design by:
Rachel Lopez
www.r2cdesign.com

Interior Design by:
Chris Treccani
www.3dogcreative.net

Editing: Cynthia Kane
Author's photo courtesy of Caroline White Photography
http://carolinewhitephotography.com
Illustrations by Sandra Jockus

In an effort to support local communities, raise awareness and funds, Morgan James Publishing donates a percentage of all book sales for the life of each book to Habitat for Humanity Peninsula and Greater Williamsburg.

Get involved today! Visit
www.MorganJamesBuilds.com

Dedication

For my mother,
who never acted like there was an upper limit,
so I never saw one.

Table of Contents

Introduction
What Are You *Really* Waiting for?

The writing is on the wall – if you want to kill it in your business and bring your message to the world, video is how you're going to get there. By 2017, 74% of all Internet traffic will be video. Video isn't just the primary form of content for the future, it also blows away all other formats for reach and conversion. 4x as many consumers would rather watch a video about a product than read about it. Social video generates 1200% more shares than text and images combined. Video on a landing page can increase conversions by 80% or more. Web searches bring 41% more traffic to those using video compared to those who aren't.

It's clear that *not* having a video component to your business and marketing will be a serious disadvantage going forward. Ten years ago an entrepreneur could get massive traction on blog posts and text-only email marketing, but that ship has sailed as results from those forms of content continue to become more and more anemic. Probably, I'm not telling you anything you don't already know, and yet, I'm guessing you've put off doing video consistently or at all thus far. Because the thing about video is, *there's nowhere to hide.*

Imagine your video series promoting your new program is launching next week. How ready do you feel? Yes, you'd have to design content for it. If you've been blogging and posting on social media you already know how to talk to your audience, so that's nothing new. Sure, you'd have to either figure out how to shoot the video or hire someone who knows how. Deciding what to learn on YouTube or through courses and what to hire someone to do has likely been a part of your business since the very beginning when you were designing your logo and building your website. The information is out there and truth be told, with modern technology it's just not that complicated.

The single factor that stands in the way of feeling ready to shoot those videos next week, the one that separates video from all other forms of content, is that you will have to show up on camera and be seen as the face of your business. Which means you will need to know exactly how to style your hair, makeup and clothing to send the right visual messages to your audience to let them know that you are the person who can solve their problem. Your appearance will have a huge impact on the success of your business and yet, you don't exactly remember proper grooming being covered in B-School.

The need to master your image and look well groomed in your business is especially tangible for women. Studies have shown that for men, most of the benefits of being attractive in their careers (which are present but much more moderate than those for women) are distributed mostly on the basis of their genetics with a small extra bump for good grooming. For women, however, the difference in income that can be attributed to attractiveness (which is much greater than what men experience) has much more to do with grooming than the features they were born with. Unfair though this may seem, and indeed on many level is, it's also a double edged sword, because it means that while you will have to spend more time and energy on your appearance than a man might, you also have the ability to leverage your appearance to control your results.

The amount you have to gain may be more than you imagine. For a woman with average features, the difference between being poorly groomed and being well groomed can mean the difference between an average of $20,000 a year and an average of $35,000 a year. Almost double, at the cost of knowing which lipstick to wear and how to pick out a skirt that flatters her hips. No liquid diets, no Botox, just learning how to dress to present yourself well is enough to make a huge impact. Of course it isn't fair that your business will be judged on the basis of how flattering your hairstyle is instead of your expertise and experience.

Unfortunately, the fairness or unfairness of this system doesn't have an impact on the truth of the matter – for the foreseeable future, appearance counts, and it counts a lot.

In this book, you will be introduced to key knowledge and information that will enable you to step up and become the face of your business. You will learn how to become one of "those women" who always look incredible in their videos (and it won't involve a diet or a facelift). You will have the tools you need to develop an unforgettable signature style that makes your ideal client both want to work with you and be willing to pay top dollar for the privilege. When you look like the expert you truly are, there is no glass ceiling.

You may be thinking these things are impossible *for you.* You're not pretty enough, thin enough, or young enough. You should probably just crawl back behind that tiny headshot on a corner of your blog. But another voice, no matter how small, believes you are destined for greatness. That's why you're here right now. If you follow the method laid out in this book, you will master your image and be equipped to take your business as far as you want it to go with you front and center all the way.

Most people believe that dressing well and looking good are about following formulas and trying to match up to an ideal. But most of the world's most legendary beauties with the most iconic personal styles didn't adhere to an ideal and they didn't follow formulas. Instead, they threw the rule book away and created a new set of rules in their own image. Possibly the most celebrated beauty of all time, Audrey Hepburn, thought of herself as "a good mixture of defects." She felt she was too skinny (yes, there was a time when that might have been considered a flaw) and that her nose and feet were too big and her breasts too small. Instead of trying to hide these features however, she played into them. Rather than dressing like a person who saw herself as gawky and boyish, she dressed herself as an elegantly ethereal Pixie. In the context of the right clothing, hairstyle and makeup, her litheness and lack of curves became sublime delicacy, and her oversized facial features gained a youthful mischievousness audiences couldn't (and still can't) get enough of.

I can promise you that if Audrey tried to conceal her "flaws," her image would not have reached the legendary status it now enjoys. And yet, the vast majority of image consultants focus on teaching clients how to do exactly that. That mentality may make the client feel comfortable, but it always leads to encouraging the client to hide and diminish their uniqueness, which is not going to get more eyes on your videos. As a counterpoint to such rigid conformist philosophies, a movement towards wearing whatever one likes has arisen to equally disastrous results (more on that in Chapter 1).

Even with my background in fashion design, I didn't always know what the right solution was. Back when I was completing my degree at Parsons School of Design, I remember my closet being such a mess of different ideas that it was almost impossible to get dressed for school in the morning without having every last piece of my wardrobe laundered. I sure had followed my heart when I was shopping for all of those things, then found I could hardly make a coherent outfit.

I was paranoid about anyone seeing either my belly or my cleavage (as if anyone would miss them anyhow!) and so I wore mostly tent dresses that completely obscured my figure and made me look bigger than I was. Many days I ended up feeling so awful in what I had on that I wanted to hide under a desk if I couldn't go home and change. All my fashion knowledge didn't get me the signature style I dreamed of. I could give you a decade-by-decade tour of the fashions of Europe in the 19th century as well as the highlights from that season's runway shows, but I couldn't get dressed day-to-day without constant drama.

Fast forward to a couple years after graduation, when I started to work as a costume designer. I noticed something odd as I worked with one director after another to create their vision of their characters. Usually, when a male director imagines the lead heroine of his film, he imagines her as his personal "dream girl" (yeah, go ahead and roll your eyes, I sure did a whole lot). The description he gives of the character and what he imagines her wearing will follow suit. However, the casting department will select the best actress for the role, and nine times out of ten, outside of very broad stroke qualifications like being the right age and having the right hair color, the actress does not match with the directors imaginary picture of the character. Imagine the director thinks of the character as Grace Kelly, and instead casts Sandra Bullock. The problem was, they would always still want me to dress Sandra in Grace's clothes. Intuitively, I knew it wouldn't work, and each time this happened I would explain to the director that we needed to dress *this* actress as the character, not the one in his fantasy.

One day while doing research on something unrelated online, I came across some information on personal styling from the middle of the last century. In it was clearly stated what I had already discovered through my work as a costume designer – **the simplest, clearest most effective way to communicate an individual's full visual potential is to dress her like what she already looks like**. When phrased in the context of personal styling instead of costume design, suddenly everything clicked as to why I had never been able to perfect my own personal style. I was trying to dress myself as if I didn't look like me, or as if somehow the clothing could make me look like someone else (or in my case, a wide array of someone elses depending on the day). It took some time to adjust my wardrobe, but the feedback was almost immediate when I did.

Even in my dark days of dressing when I would frequently want to cry about the outfit I had on, people still fussed over my style and thought I looked cool, but it was *nothing* like what I experience now. Frequently when meeting a client in the large public square outside my studio, they recognize me in a crowd even when they've never seen me before and don't know what I look like. My wardrobe identifies me as the person who knows how to put herself together and can solve my client's problem. And even better, I am free from the drama around my wardrobe that used to plague my life day in and day out, and I know I can dress beautifully and feel confident for any occasion.

I knew soon after I discovered this information that I had to share it with as many people as would listen. I chatted up all my girlfriends about it, who eagerly agreed to be early test subjects, and before long I was advising strangers online who wanted to achieve what I had. Five years later, I had built a business helping hundreds and hundreds of women discover the tools necessary to master their image.

I have developed a process that helps women step up as the face of their business on video and it involves defining their signature style and learning to master their own image. This book will walk you through the exact process, which happens in two phases - the discovery phase and the implementation phase.

Discovery Phase

We begin by defining your appearance goals. Most women who set out to improve their image for their business don't have specific goals in place, and so unfortunately they fail before they begin. Then, we will get in touch with your deepest desires around your personal style, so we can incorporate them in the final result for a signature style that feels right. After this, we discover your Image Archetype and personal coloring – the design that you were born with (and its incredible, unique properties) that we will be using as a template for the design of your clothing. As the final step in the discovery phase, we will put all of these pieces together to create your own Signature Style Manifesto – the code by which you will shop and dress to become the face of your business.

Implementation Phase

The first step in the implementation phase will be delving into your wardrobe to get a lay of the land and create a plan to move it towards your Manifesto. Once you have made a plan, you'll be ready to learn to shop with intention for the pieces that move you towards your goals. Finally, you will learn my tips and tricks for putting all of the pieces together to create incredible, camera-ready outfits that fully express the vision laid out in your manifesto.

I'm not going to lie to you, this process will require you to put in the work and commit to seeing it through. I can guide you through every step of the way, but only you have the power to master your image and become the face of your business. Those stylish women you see on video killing it in their businesses didn't get that way by accident, and neither will you. However, if you follow the steps in this process and do the work, you will end up with a camera ready signature style that will allow you to step out from behind the curtain and take your business as far as you can imagine. Now, let's get started.

Chapter 1
Dress As If

My Story

I was in the sixth grade, enjoying the traditional trip to the local Friendly's after a school dance when one of the coolest, most popular boys in my class arrived to my table. With him, he carried a pile of crunched up small bills collected from about half the boys in the class. He informed me with a smirk that this money (about 60 dollars) was intended to pay me for a particular sexual favor. Never mind that I had no experience in the topic at hand, my outfit that evening, which showed a small bit of my ever-growing cleavage, had informed them that I would be available for such a service. I want to say that I was disgusted, but the shameful truth is that while I acted outwardly incensed, I was secretly delighted. Up until that moment I had heard endless feedback from these same boys that my body was too big and fat to ever be appealing, offensive to their sensibilities and hardly worthy of existing. And yet, suddenly they had found a use for it. Already before I ever donned the dress I wore that night, my own inner value of my body had been worn down to the point where on some level, $60 felt like a fair price. No wonder I spent most of my life desperately praying to magically have a different body.

I'm not going to sit here and tell you that I am 100% right with my body and that all of those wounds are completely healed. What I can tell you is that decades of trying to will myself into loving myself didn't work. What did work, was acting as if. After discovering the tools in this book, I started to dress myself *as if* I accepted my body by consciously choosing to lean into my physical design instead of struggling desperately against it. Immediately, things started to shift. I stopped standing in dressing rooms, ready to cry because none of the clothes I loved fit right or looked good on me. I stopped spending hours each week taking things off and putting them back on trying to slap together an acceptable outfit for the day. I stopped trying to force my body to be something it wasn't and started dressing what it actually was. And most shocking of all, the world did not implode. People did not line up in the streets to point and laugh and put me back in my place. In fact, quite the opposite. I started being received better by others, and somehow I started feeling more satisfied with my reflection.

Acting as if I loved my body put everyone at ease, as if my appearance said "I know who I am and I'm ok with it," and that by acknowledging the elephant in the room, it disappeared.

You don't get to choose how other people react to you. No matter how beautiful you are or how well dressed, there is always going to be someone who believes how you look is not ok, and they may not hesitate to say so. Just look at the social media pages of virtually any female public figure if you want proof. What you do get to choose is how you present yourself. You can choose to hide yourself and pander to every bit of criticism, real or imagined. You can hide behind a blog with a blurry selfie hidden halfway down the about page. You've probably already proven to yourself that will work, up to a point. Some clients will come and some of them will be helped. Or, you can choose to show up looking like the person you were born to be.

Fourth Time's the Charm

When I met Tina, she had already tried and failed to refine her image with no less than three stylists. Some consultants would see that as the mark of a difficult client, I saw it as a testament to her remarkable resilience. These experiences had mostly confirmed what she already thought about herself – she had no taste and didn't seem to be able to cultivate any, and that her physical self was irreparably flawed to boot. If it weren't for her fierce determination to show up in her business and share her message with the world, Tina might have given up. And yet, somehow deep inside she believed that she could overcome these obstacles if she could just find the right guide, and when a mutual friend recommended me, she booked an appointment.

My work with Tina started as I virtually always do, with an analysis of her coloring, body and features. This process probably sounds about as appealing as a root canal to most women, but

Tina experienced something interesting. When I described what I saw without identifying any particular feature as either an asset or a flaw, she suddenly felt lighter. Her body wasn't right or wrong, it simply *was*. When I went on to describe which clothing would be most harmonious with her own physical design, she started to get excited. You see, Tina didn't actually have bad taste, and there is nothing wrong with the way she looks. Tina is a Pixie Image Archetype, (which you will read more about in Chapter 3) with a naturally animated and explosive personality and physical appearance, and her taste expressed that.

Think of a sort of Ellen DeGeneres of women's finance. No wonder she failed to submit to her previous stylist's ideas about quiet elegance and dressing her age! The clothes they picked were indeed chic and sophisticated *for someone else*. On Tina they were heavy, serious, and lethargic, which translated to looking frumpy, sloppy, and older than she needed to look. Together, we chose clothing that was crisp, playful and unexpected, just like she is. Not only does Tina look stylish and beautiful in her new clothes, they express her incredible energy and spirit and position her with her audience as a bold rebel willing to break paradigms to empower them. By dressing *as if*, Tina is able to leverage her visual potential to attract clients and followers who need her message and are ready to be led by her.

What *Doesn't* Work

If you want to dress for your highest potential, attract clients and look incredible on video, there are two extremely pervasive philosophies that you must abandon. I call these methods the Correct & Conceal Method and the Follow Your Heart method. Both have good intentions and sincere merit, but both suffer from an inherently flawed perspective that prevents the user from getting the results they dream about.

The Correct and Conceal Method

The Correct and Conceal Method usually sounds something like "If you're an apple, wear X to correct your Y," or "If you're a pear wear X to conceal your Y." Most mainstream makeover shows (What Not to Wear, for example) and most popular women's magazine (Cosmopolitan, et. al.) espouse this method. The basic premise is that there is one correct way to look and it is medium, moderate, and symmetrical. Any features that deviate from this ideal model are seen as flaws that need to be either hidden or corrected. There are, in fact some merits to this perspective. First, it's helpful that this method at the very least starts with the idea that the styles that are most ideal for us will be flattering to our body or somehow related to it. Also, dozens of scientific studies do show that we find symmetry in other human beings attractive, so there's no denying that there's some merit there. Of course, scientific studies also show that men will choose a silhouette of a woman with a waist so small she couldn't actually exist due to a lack of space for organs over one with a slightly more subtle waist-to-hip ratio, but somehow I doubt that one pans out exactly that way in real life.

From my perspective, the idea of dressing in a way that constantly fixates on one's "flaws" feels particularly grim. Imagine going to your closet each morning and thinking "time to put on my X to conceal my Y!"… It's depressing, and it breeds a constant reinforcement of the idea that our bodies are wrong. It may be you're alright with stoically facing your "flaws" day after day in order to achieve the goal of a flattering and attractive figure. However, you will still be disappointed by this method *because it doesn't work.*

How could that be so? Well, quite simply, because human perception doesn't work the way this method claims. The fundamental principle behind the Correct and Conceal Method is that you can create certain visual illusions to trick the viewer into thinking you look different than how you actually look. I'm sorry to be the one to break it to you, but people have eyes and they can see you. No amount of dressing in a long vertical block of color is going to convince onlookers that you are in fact 5'7" and not actually 5'2". Even with high heels, you're a 5'2" woman wearing high heels. Whether or not you believe it's ok to be 5'2", that is reality. In case you are thinking that you may at least look a bit longer or slimmer by following this method, let me assure you, you will get the exact opposite result you are hoping for. Human beings see relatively, not objectively.

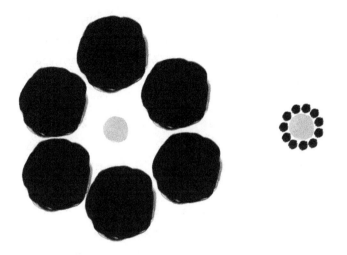

Let's pretend the grey dot above is a petite woman who would like to appear less petite. The two grey dots are in fact identical in size. By following the Correct and Conceal Method, we would do things like put a giant head to toe block of color on her in efforts to make her look bigger. What happens to the small grey dot when you put proportionately huge dots next to it? It looks *even smaller.* By surrounding herself with small effects and proportions instead, as in the picture with the small dots, she appears bigger.

The reason she doesn't do this herself is because she is afraid. What she fears is looking tiny, childlike, insignificant, not worthy of being listened to. Unfortunately, when she allows her fear to control her choices and chooses large proportions in hopes of somehow absorbing their impact, she diminishes herself, looks like a kid playing dress-up, and gets more of what she fears. If you want to become the face of your business and create a platform to reach thousands or millions with your message, you will not get there by trying to hide or fix yourself. Only by embracing and moving towards your physical self instead of away from it will you be able to unleash your visual potential and make your mark on the world.

The Follow Your Heart Method

But what about what's inside, isn't that what counts? Isn't the sum total of my personality, my spirit, my values, my expertise and my message what's most important? In short, yes. Philosophically speaking, like most people I believe that, as John Locke said, the core of personal identity is made up of sameness of consciousness. This is the principal on which the Follow Your Heart Method rests. Basically, the idea is that since it's what is inside that counts, we should dress in a way that expresses our inner self. Usually this advice involves journaling about oneself, identifying style muses, making mood boards and the like. These tools can be helpful (in fact we will use some later), but on their own don't tend to pan out as a practical solution that will have you dressed and feeling confident for your video shoot next week.

Consciousness is vast. You are many things, doubtless some of them are contradictory, which is part of the magic of you as a human being. You may need a different wardrobe to dress the person you were on Tuesday than the one you chose for Saturday's you. But you only have one physical body, and that physical body has some finite qualities. In this lifetime, your eyes are not likely to get further apart or closer together. The length of your femur, the width of your hip bones, and that particular way your mouth tilts when you're amused is probably going to stay the same as long as you continue to draw breath. Of course you will change somewhat, you are older or younger, you weigh more or less, you give birth, you grow old. Yet your physical self stays the same more than it changes. In this sense, your physical person is an inherent and inextricable, and yes, authentic part of you. It also happens to be the part of you that we're going to be putting clothing on. Fashion is a somewhat unique art form in that a garment isn't complete until it is hanging on a body. The relationship between your physical self and the end result of a particular look can no more be broken than that between a work of art and the canvas it is painted upon. If you are choosing a lifestyle, a place to live, or your life's work you should definitely consider your inner self far more than your outer self. Your personality, goals and desires do matter. But you are not just a brain in a jar, and your physical person is essential to bringing your message to the people who most need to hear it.

Authenticity is important, but so is working with the raw materials encoded in your DNA. If you want to create a personal style that expresses you to your full potential, there is really only one thing you need to do – repeat yourself. Simply put, that means that the colors, shapes, design lines and proportions that already exist in you, are the ones you must wear. Beauty is not something that you need to source from the outside, it is simply what you are when you remove distortion or dilution. You already effortlessly experience this truth whenever you bear witness to Nature in its unadulterated raw form. Nature is the ultimate designer. As clever as we can be as human beings, we will never best her for sheer awe and soul-deep impact. You were woven from the same fabric as the Grand Canyon, the Rocky Mountains, and the beaches of Antigua. Your eye color is as perfect for your skin tone as a clownfish is for the coral reef it lives in. Your cheekbones, nose and jaw are as carefully arranged as the branches on an evergreen. Your visual potential and the potential to use it to make an impact on the world is literally your birthright.

If you're like most of my clients, you are probably experiencing some resistance right now. You might be thinking, surely if I can just find the right combination of wardrobe pieces, I can hide my flaws. Or surely if I just dress how I feel on the inside, my message will come through.

What you are feeling is a perfectly normal reaction. Every advertisement you have ever seen has first tried to convince you that you are flawed so that you will then feel the need to buy their product to fix yourself. You have also probably heard these messages repeated from your mother, your girlfriends, and even total strangers out in the world. Your friends and family are not out to get you, they are just victims of the same comparative beauty model that has been and for the foreseeable future will be drilled into you at every opportunity.

These two methods aren't without merit, but they are incomplete and in the end rely on some fatally flawed assumptions. I'm going to show you a new way to approach your image that will have you feeling comfortable and confident in your own skin, looking more gorgeous than you ever imagined was possible, and attracting viewers that connect with you on a deep level and turn into clients more effortlessly than these old ways ever could.

Part One:
Discovery

Chapter 2
Set Your Image Goals

In order to achieve your image goals, first you have to set them. This may sound unbearably obvious, but most of my clients come to me in hopes of accomplishing something pretty amorphous. If you set out to "dress your best," you probably will not get there, because it's too non-specific to know when you've achieved it.

My suggestion is to start by making a running list, in no particular order, of all of the occasions you have to dress for. Try to make them relatively specific. For example, if you need to both meet with clients one on one and shoot video those should be separate occasions rather than just "work."

While this book is designed to help you master your image to take your business to the next level, I also highly,

highly suggest that you include the occasions in your life that have nothing to do with work. Do you go on dates with your husband twice a month? Take your kids to the park? Write those down. I can assure you that if you are perfectly polished for only the hours on the clock when you are actively being seen by clients and a wreck the rest of the time, you will still feel like you have a problem. Marie Forleo, whom I have learned much from, frequently says, "How you do one thing is how you do everything," and in the case of your wardrobe it definitely applies. From now on, you are going to give yourself the gift of looking like you give a shit even if you're writing a blog post alone in your living room.

You can choose whether to include things like walking the dog, sleeping, or working out. If you live in the country and just stand out on your back porch while the dogs runs out you might not need the "easy to throw on but still chic" looks someone who lives in an urban setting would prefer (at least not for that particular purpose). Many of my clients find that once they start dressing to express their highest visual potential, they want to keep doing it all the time, including their PJs and exercise clothes.

Once you have your list, you will want to think about what your needs are for each of the occasions listed. Some of these needs should be abstract, including both how you want to feel in your clothes for that occasion, or how you would like to be seen by those around you. For occasions related to your business, you will want to consider how your ideal target viewer needs you to show up in order to believe you as the person who can solve her problem. Entire books can and have been written about how to step into your ideal target viewer's shoes, so I won't go into it here, but if you haven't worked out who she is and what her problem is in her words, focusing some time there before continuing this exercise will be important. Remember to separate goals that matter to *you* from what will matter to *her*. Some of my clients also wish to extend a similar courtesy to their husbands, children, or friends for more personal occasions, so if this appeals to you, you may include it. Other goals should be concrete, such as a certain number of outfits you will need or a plan for your hair and makeup. Nothing is out of bounds, even if it feels a little bit random or you are not sure how it will play out in how you are dressing. If it's coming up, write it down.

Let's say I need to dress myself for a 3-video series I will be creating to launch a new program. I might start with the specifics – I will need three camera-appropriate outfits that work from the waist up sitting down, and I will need to decide how I want my hair and makeup to be done and how it will be done (by myself, or someone else). Then, I can move on to the abstract goals – I want to show up for my viewers as warm, compassionate, and glamorous, and I want to feel calm and confident. Now, I will have a way of knowing exactly when I have achieved these goals and I won't get sucked into endless searching or wondering if there's a better thing out there I haven't found yet. Go through each occasion you have noted down and create specific goals for yourself. It's fine if many sections sound similar, and it's also fine if they sound very contradictory. We will sort all that out later, so don't feel pressured to make it make too much sense just yet.

To give you an example of how this might look, let's check out my client Elise's goals. Elise is a scientist-turned-aesthetician who created her own skincare line of results-driven, scientifically backed products. As you will see, her business requires her to wear a few different hats which each demand a somewhat different presentation that will need to be accounted for.

Elise's Goals
Professional

1. Client Appointments in Studio (6 days per week, worn primarily while sitting under an apron) Ideal client is a woman of means age 50 who wants to look younger and eliminate acne and acne scarring and is hoping to find the right professional to just take care of it all for her. She needs Elise to be credible, knowledgeable, and trustworthy. Elise wants to feel polished, but still conversational and casual.

2. Presentations (Once per month, given in various locations to audience of potential clients) Ideal audience member is the same woman as her ideal client for her practice. Elise prefers to give off a more formal impression for these occasions than she would in her appointments.

3. B2B Presentations (4 times per year at vendor shows) Ideal client is an aesthetician age 30 who is trying to distinguish her business from the pack with the right methods and products and who realizes there's a ton of vital information she never learned in school. She needs Elise to be confident and effective, a leader who stands out that she can look up to as a mentor. Elise wants to feel polished but also distinctive and unique.

4. Informational Videos and Facebook Live (Intermittent, targeting ideal clients for her aesthetics practice) More or less the same as number 2, but with special attention to how things read on camera

5. Live Televised Sales (Intermittent, filmed at the network's studio) The network has agreed upon a similar Ideal client to Elise's own model, except this woman is slightly younger (age 40), with a tighter budget and still hoping to identify the right products on her own. She needs Elise to be a knowledgeable professional who can explain what products work and why in a way that's easy to understand and apply. Elise wants to be sure to conform to the networks aesthetic, which is clean and conservative with a little pop while still looking like herself. She also has guidelines from the network detailing their dos and don'ts for being filmed there that she must comply with.

Personal

1. Casual Dinners out and errands around town (2 times per week) Elise rarely needs to get very dressed up for her personal life and can use the same type of outfit for most occasions. She wants to feel pulled together enough to be comfortable bumping into anyone while she's out and about, and she doesn't mind being the most dressed up person in the grocery store.

2. Formal (2 times per year, a wedding or other party with friends and family) Elise is happy to step out and look distinctive and unique if possible, but mainly wants

to look elegant in a gown that flatters her without spending too much since these occasions come up rarely.

That's it for Elise, but don't worry if you have more or less. My average client has five or six separate occasions for each professional and personal, so Elise is somewhat unusual in that sense. The point is to cover all the bases that will be required in order for the signature style we are going to create to work for you.

Chapter 3
Get in Touch with Your Desires

Once you have become clear on your goals, there's one more thing you need to get in touch with on the inside before we start talking about the outside – your desires. You may be thinking that you don't care what you wear so long as you look good in your videos and get clients! However, experience tells me that you have an extremely honed in idea of what appeals to you to wear. You just don't realize it because you use this sense of what you like and dislike as easily as you inhale and exhale. How we desire to appear is so deeply linked with our identity at the deepest level that it can become an insurmountable wall between us and the amazing work we want to do. In short, do not skip this step!

This process involves making a mood board using images that you will source. You can use any method you like, but I suggest creating a Pinterest account if you don't already have one (it's free) and starting a secret board just for this exercise. If learning a new application will stand in your way, you are totally free to sit down with a stack of fashion magazines, scissors, and glue. Be sure that at the end you will be able to collect the images in a way that allows you to see them more or less all at once. Do whatever seems like it would be fun to you and don't get stuck on the method.

I want you to look for images of the clothing you would wear if you had no budget and would be guaranteed that no matter what you choose you will be totally comfortable physically, appropriate for any occasion and you will look good in it. The only qualification is that assuming all that were true is that you would actually put it on and leave the house in it. You are encouraged to also choose images of hair, makeup and accessories that meet this criteria, but try to avoid the distraction of choosing photos just because you like the picture itself or think the model is pretty. Try to avoid judging or filtering your own choices as much as possible. If you are questioning whether an image should be on your board, close your eyes and imagine that you look down and find yourself wearing that outfit. Knowing that in this vision, the outfit flatters you perfectly and is totally comfortable on, are you thrilled to be wearing it? You will know. Between 20 and 50 images is the right amount, if you have more go back and edit down to the best ones.

When you are satisfied with the board, I want you to look at the board as a whole as if you were a fashion designer and this were the mood board for your next collection. Try to find a few themes and motifs that capture the essence of your board. For example, my own boards usually have themes like whimsical, sophisticated, and luxurious, and feature black, white, red and pink and a high level of embellishment and garment detail as motifs.

If you are having trouble connecting your images to one another, look at a few of your most favorite and ask yourself what you like **about** that particular item. You should start to see patterns emerging. Don't even try to evaluate them on the basis of how they will work on your body or in your business yet, anything goes right now. There's a reason why we are doing this before we talk about how to repeat your physical self, as we talked about last chapter. Ideally, you will have at least 5 and no more than 10 themes or motifs, including a mixture of both.

Let's check back in with Elise, who we met in Chapter 2. When I help clients identify their themes, I generally use 2-3 words for each to help clarify concepts which could be interpreted a number of different ways. Go ahead and define your themes any way that feels right to you. As you can see below, Elise's desires do repeat certain concepts from her goals, but we also uncover some new dimensions that more fully flesh out what signature style would feel right to her.

Elise's Themes

1. Bold/Powerful
2. Clean/Sleek
3. Tailored/Architectural/Graphic
4. Modern (contemporary)
5. Masculine/Feminine

6. Luxury/High-End
7. Polished/Stylized

Additional notes: strong thematic use of black & white contrast and solid jewel tones

Your goals and desires are a critical part of your journey from fashion rookie to camera ready woman of style. When I first met my client Sara, she was struggling daily with her image, despite her enviable physical design (standing nearly 6' tall, with bodacious curves, never ending legs, and delicate facial bones, she strikes an impressive figure to say the least.) She seemed to be having a disconnect between what she thought she was supposed to wear, and what she *wanted* to wear.

When I reviewed the desire board that Sara made, I was able to identify some very clear themes and motifs. First of all, I noticed that Sara had a penchant for minimalism. The quiet boldness of minimal lines expressed her gentle personality and made her feel (and look) calm and confident in her business, which focused on bringing her client more ease in their lives and businesses. On a similar note, she preferred neutral colors and shades of blue-green, which offered a natural feeling in line with her message. Last, the images she chose had a pervasive sense of nostalgia captured in styles that subtly nodded to the past, perhaps a visual antidote to the aggressive hustle towards the next thing she alleviates for her clients. After determining this, I both completely understood why she was struggling, and was excited to show her just how to correct course.

In her mind, Sara thought that because she looked like a Scandinavian Sophia Loren, she was supposed to wear something along the lines of a Versace runway show – colorful, flashy, ornate, and over the top. While these styles would absolutely flatter Sara, they were out of alignment with her inner self and how she wanted to show up in the world. Fortunately, her themes and motifs fit perfectly with a more creative interpretation of her physicality.

Now that you have spent some time getting in touch with your desires, you have a clear vision of what needs to be included in your signature style in order for it to feel exciting and satisfying. This will allow you to go forward making choices without being distracted by every passing whim, but also without feeling deprived of what you truly crave.

Your goals and desires are not enough to guide your style choices on their own, but as we continue you'll see that they play a very important role in crafting your unique signature style. The next step in the process? Discovering your image archetype!

Chapter 4
Discover Your Archetype

N ow that you have gotten in touch with your goals and desires, you are ready to understand your physical design so you can start stepping into your signature style. Learning to repeat your own physical design (as we discussed in Chapter 1) is a critical step in mastering your image.

So what is an Image Archetype? Essentially, it's a combination of shape, line, scale and proportion that creates a conceptual style. To give you an idea of what I mean, imagine that you are tasked with decorating a log cabin. What kinds of furnishings would you look for? I'm guessing that you would probably choose something rustic and organic looking with a casual and cozy vibe, regardless of your preferences in interior décor. On the other hand, I doubt you will have chosen hyper modern furnishings made of metal and molded plastic fit for a black tie affair. Possibly there's an interior decorator somewhere who could make that look fabulous, but the easiest and most logical choice would be to furnish a log cabin like...a log cabin. Not only does this create an incredibly harmonious and attractive end result with minimal training and effort required, it also allows us to capitalize off of the best elements of the log cabin that are already there without having to create some new appeal from scratch.

If you haven't guessed, the log cabin in need of the right décor is a metaphor for a person in need of the right clothing. The quickest, easiest, most effective way to dress a person is to dress them to look like themselves. So just as we have styles such as Midcentury Modern or Colonial in interior design, in fashion we have Image Archetypes.

In my analysis of hundreds of women (thousands including those who pass me on the street each day), I have identified ten Image Archetypes that, while possessing the flexibility for millions of variations, describe any given individual.

What follows are descriptions of each of the ten Image Archetypes. You will find their physical characteristics described near the beginning of each section. Before you read through them, spend some time examining your physical features while standing in front of a full-length mirror in clothing that does not obstruct your body. If you try to recall in your mind what your body looks like, your brain will undoubtedly fill in some gaps incorrectly. Of course you probably already know how tall you are. If you don't, be sure to measure and find out.

This will give you a general impression of your scale. Other factors to consider to determine your scale are the breadth of your shoulders, the length of your limbs, and the size of your hands and feet. Write down your observations. Next, draw your attention to the overall shape of your figure. Imagine you were to snap a picture and cut out your silhouette. As you move along the torso, do the lines move more in and out or more up and down? Most women have some curvature, the question is whether those horizontal movements are more prominent than the verticals. Finally, draw your attention to your face. Notice the bone structure, what shapes are there, and what the topography is like – are there high peaks and low valleys or are things flatter and more softly transitioned? Also make note of the shape and size of the eyes and mouth, as well as the tautness or softness of the cheek and the texture of the hair.

Take deep breaths and try to distance yourself from the person in the mirror. Describe her features to yourself as if she is another person, one you love very much. Be honest, but not unkind to her. Once you have observed your physical characteristics, proceed to the following Image Archetype descriptions, stopping only briefly to read the overall description and physical features before moving on to the next one. Access the quiet part within you and ask yourself for each description whether that is you. If you try to determine this analytically by matching yourself exactly to every single facet of a description, you will succeed in confusing yourself and not find your Image Archetype. Choose the one that fits best and feels right without needing every single factor to line up. Most of my clients already know their Image Archetype at some level before I walk them through the process of discerning it.

Whatever you do, do NOT survey your sister, your mother, your husband or your girlfriend. They don't know. They have not lived a lifetime in your body and they are not qualified to be responsible for your appearance decisions. Your lived experience in your body and your unhindered powers of perception are sufficient to solve this problem.

If you're having trouble choosing your archetype, try asking yourself a few questions. Which part of you never fits in ready-made clothing? What expression do you most frequently catch yourself making without realizing? What do strangers always comment on? If you have no idea which of these might pertain to you... STOP READING!!! And instead, go to my detailed video primer on determining your type www.thefaceofthebusiness.com/toolkit. Once you have really honed down on your type, go ahead and read the appropriate section.

The Queen

Glamorous and powerful, the epitome of the avant-garde. You have an aura of raw power around you, looking at you feels a bit like looking a jaguar in the eyes. Your stature gives you a built-in pedestal, which creates an apartness from the crowd, and an air of awe and mystery.

Features: Large scale angular bone structure, linear body type, angular facial bone structure and facial features. Usually tall (5'5"+) with long arms and legs and has narrow bone structure. Hands and feet are typically long but narrow. Generally lithe, though like any type may be overweight, and if so excess flesh will gravitate to the lower body. Like all women the queen may have curves but tends to be more up and down than in and out. She has angular or prominent facial bone structure (brow bone, nose, cheekbone, and jawline) with high peaks and low valleys to their topography. Her facial features (eyes, lips) are more linear (like parallel lines) than rounded (circle or half circle).

Celebrity Examples: Lauren Bacall, Anjelica Houston, Iman, Tilda Swinton, Cate Blanchett

Alternate variations: the Elf, the Baroness, the Film Noir Heroine

Superpower: The Queen is raw power incarnate. Her physical self is extreme and so is the impact she makes. The most dynamic, high fashion styles imaginable are merely her normal baseline.

Kryptonite: Playing small. There is nothing average or under the radar about this woman and anything less than bold extremes will subtract from her superpower.

Historical Periods: Ancient Egypt, Edwardian Era, 1940s, 1980s Avant-garde

What The Queen Wears Best

Shapes: The long and slender rectangle and long acute triangle are the core shapes for the Queen. Sharply angular shapes with crisp edges repeat her innate design best.

Silhouette: Elongation is the key to maximizing the Queen's bold physicality. Lines should always be more vertical than horizontal. She should avoid silhouettes that are cropped, color blocked, or fit-and-flare.

Coordination style: One consolidated statement. She should avoid fragmenting herself with too many small, competitive design elements.

Fit & Fabrics: The Queen's garments should sit slim to the body and be relatively tailored. The ideal fabrics for her are smooth, sleek, and structured.

Color: Colors should be coordinated, limited in number and ideally will be worn in long, head-to-toe blocks. Neutrals and bold colors both work well providing they flatter her coloring, but she should choose one or the other as the primary scheme for each outfit.

Motifs: Patterns and design details for the Queen should be bold, angular, edgy and modern. Allocation should be extreme, either Spartan minimalism or over the top avant-garde embellishment.

Tops: Necklines should be angular with clean edges. V-neck, Jewel neck, keyhole, slot neck, asymmetrical, cross-over and halter work well as do necklines that sweep upwards such as turtlenecks, mandarin collars, and man-tailored collars. Sleeves should either have dramatic sweep or be slim with high and tight armholes.

Skirts: Long and column shaped. At minimum they should reach the base of the knee with no maximum length.

Pants: Straight and trouser-cut with a half or full break or slim cigarette with no break.

Dresses: Sculptural, long columns or elongated, body-skimming shapes.

Jackets & Cardigans: Hip-length blazer with sharp lapels. Sleek, long cardigans that sit close to the body.

Outerwear: Bold and sweeping tailored coats with oversize collars, dramatic hoods or unusual asymmetrical shaping.

Jewelry & Accessories: Big, unusual, and extremely glamorous. Make a statement or leave it at home.

Shoes: Sharply pointed and streamlined, like elegant weapons. Heels over 3" otherwise flat.

Bags: Sculptural and large scale. Uncommon shapes and materials.

Hair: Sculptural and unique, often extremely long or extremely short. Asymmetry is a plus.

Makeup: Polished and graphic, i.e. cut creases, winged liner, contouring, matte lipstick. Create these effect with shades that are appropriate to your natural coloring.

Keywords: Large scale, bold, sharply angular, unique, elongated, extreme, sculptural.

The Goddess

Mysterious and dangerous, the epitome of over-the-top, non-stop glamour. Your aura of mystique draws people into your world like a vortex. The powerful presence of your large scale, angular bone structure paired with the undeniable sex appeal of a very curvaceous body creates a thrilling impression like no other.

Features: Large scale angular bone structure and facial bones with voluptuously curvy body type and rounded facial features. Usually tall (5'5"+) with long arms and legs and has narrow bone structure. Hands and feet are typically long but narrow. The goddess is generally voluptuously curvy (and will only get more so with excess weight) unless very thin. She has angular or prominent facial bone structure (brow bone, nose, cheekbone, and jawline) with high peaks and low valleys to their topography. Her facial features (eyes, lips) are more rounded (circle or half circle) than linear (like parallel lines).

Celebrity Examples: Sophia Loren, Christina Hendricks, Beyoncé, Sonam Kapoor, Rachel Weisz

Alternate variations: the Stage Diva, the Dragon Lady

Superpower: The Goddess is surrounded by a cloud of intrigue. She has power akin to that of the Queen, but shrouded in a velvet glove of mystery and sensuality. For this luxurious and glamorous woman, too much is never enough.

Kryptonite: Anything mundane. The Goddess is so extraordinary one might wonder which planet she descended from, but too much plainness might convince us to ignore her.

Historical Periods: Ancient Greece and Rome, Baroque Era, 1940s

What The Goddess Wears Best

Shapes: The elongated figure 8 and the acute triangle are the core shapes for the Goddess. A mixture of bold, rounded shapes and sharply angular shapes repeat her innate design best.

Silhouette: Flowing elongation is the key to maximizing the Goddess' bold physicality and sensual curves. Lines should always be more vertical than horizontal. She should avoid silhouettes that are cropped, color blocked, or rigidly straight.

Coordination style: One consolidated statement. She should avoid fragmenting herself with too many small, competitive design elements.

Fit & Fabrics: The Goddess' garments should have flow and drape but sit close to the body. The ideal fabrics for her are smooth, lightweight, and are either unstructured or have plenty of stretch.

Color: Colors should be coordinated, limited in number and ideally will be worn in long, head-to-toe blocks. Neutrals and bold colors both work well providing they flatter her coloring, but she should choose one or the other as the primary scheme for each outfit.

Motifs: Patterns and design details for the Goddess should be bold, lavish, and uncommon. Allocation should be extreme, either Spartan minimalism or over the top avant-garde embellishment.

Tops: Necklines should be open and soft or else high. V-neck, cowl neck, keyhole, asymmetrical, cross-over and halter work well as do necklines that sweep upwards such as turtlenecks, mandarin collars, and man-tailored collars. Sleeves should either have dramatic sweep or be slim with high and tight armholes.

Skirts: Long and tapered to the knee with plenty of drape or stretch. At minimum they should reach the base of the knee with no maximum length.

Pants: Softly draped bootcut and trouser-cut pants with a half or full break or slim skinny pants with no break.

Dresses: Grecian inspired long draped columns with waist definition or elongated, body-skimming shapes.

Jackets & Cardigans: Hip-length blazer with soft lapels. Sweeping, long cardigans with waist shaping.

Outerwear: Bold and sweeping tailored coats with oversize collars, dramatic hoods or unusual asymmetrical shaping.

Jewelry & Accessories: Big, unusual, and extremely glamorous. Make a statement or leave it at home.

Shoes: Sharply pointed and streamlined, like elegant weapons. Heels over 3" otherwise flat.

Bags: Softly draped and large scale. Uncommon shapes and materials.

Hair: Long sumptuous curls or waves with plenty of volume are ideal, though Goddesses with straight, fine hair texture can choose a sculptured short cut.

Makeup: A finished face with a mix of angles (dramatic eyeliner and brows, cut creases) and soft diffuse elements (glossy lips, blushy cheeks, shimmer and highlight) using the shades appropriate for your coloring.

Keywords: Large-scale, bold, sharply angular, curve conscious, elongated, lavish, extreme, sensual

The Muse

Fresh and unaffected, elevated with a modern edge. There is a grounded and earthy quality to you, you feel very "real," with a hint of something mysterious and very uncommon. Like a model on the catwalk, your statuesque proportions elevate you above the crowd, but your winning smile and easy approachability keep you from ever becoming distant or forbidding.

Features: Large scale, angular bone structure, linear body type, and softly angular facial bone structure and facial features. Usually tall (5'5"+) with long arms and legs and has broad bone structure. Hands and feet are large and may be either broad or long and narrow. The muse is generally lithe or muscular but like any type may be overweight, and if so excess flesh will tend to gravitate to her midsection and hips. Like all women she may have curves but she tends to be more up and down than she is in and out, especially when thin. Her facial bone structure (brow bone, nose, cheekbone, and jawline) may be broad and bluntly angular (wide with gently rolling topography) or prominent and angular (with high peaks and valleys). Her facial features (eyes, lips) are more linear (like parallel lines) than rounded (like circle or half circle).

Celebrity Examples: Lauren Hutton, Giselle, Julia Roberts, Venus Williams, Blake Lively

Alternate variations: the Off-duty Model, the California Girl, the Celebrity BFF

Superpower: The Muse epitomizes the kind of effortless cool lauded in every fashion magazine. Inherently glamorous and yet somehow approachable, she really did just wake up like that.

Kryptonite: Being too controlled or contrived. This free spirit's energy needs room to breathe and permission to go her own way.

Historical Periods: The late 1910s and 20s, the late 1960s, the 1970s

What The Muse Wears Best

Shapes: The rectangle and the square are the core shapes for The Muse. Bluntly angular shapes with softened edges repeat her innate design best.

Silhouette: Elongation is the key to maximizing the Muse's bold physicality. Lines should always be more vertical than horizontal. She should avoid silhouettes that are cropped, color blocked, or fit-and-flare.

Coordination style: An artistic mix-and-match approach conveys the casual nonchalance of the Muse best.

Fit & Fabrics: The Muse's garments should be relaxed, with plenty of drape and flow to allow for freedom of movement. The ideal fabrics for her are light and flowing or else chunky and textural.

Color: Colors that are flattering to her complexion should be mixed freely, as on a painters palette.

Motifs: Patterns and design details for the Muse should be bold, angular, organic and artistic. She may choose to pile it on or dress relatively simply, but minimalism is too controlled for her.

Tops: Necklines should be open and unconfined. Open V-necks, deep cowl necks, scoop necks, boat necks, one shoulder, asymmetrical, cross-over and halter work well as do necklines that sweep upwards such as open man-tailored collars. Sleeves may either have dramatic sweep or be relaxed with unconstricted dropped armholes.

Skirts: Long and column shaped. At minimum they should reach the base of the knee with no maximum length. Extreme minis are another option.

Pants: Straight and trouser-cut or bootleg with a half or full break.

Dresses: Relaxed columns, elongated, freely flowing shapes, or mini dresses with some drape and flow.

Jackets & Cardigans: Relaxed hip-length blazers with angular lapels. Long, free-flowing draped cardigans.

Outerwear: Bold and unstructured coats with asymmetrical, oversize collars or dramatic hoods.

Jewelry & Accessories: Big, artistic, and expressive. Unique pieces with an organic or hand-made quality.

Shoes: Substantial and funky with angular toes, or else open and bare. Heels over 3" otherwise flat.

Bags: Unstructured and large scale. Textured materials and detailing and substantial hardware.

Hair: Textured and tousled is best, like hair after a day at the beach, always with softness around the face. Those with the texture to support it may wear a very long "lion's mane", while those with finer hair may option for short cuts with plenty of layering and movement.

Makeup: Fresh and clean, always with a natural looking skin finish even when bolder effects like a bright lip or smoky eyeliner are used. Contour can be effective but keep it imperceptible to maintain the illusion. Very neutral, minimalist makeup can be used, providing the shades used are appropriate for your coloring.

Keywords: Large-scale, softly angular, elongated, eclectic, organic, effortless, substantial.

The Enchantress

Relaxed and approachable with an earthy sensuality. Your mixture of down-to-earth realness and a hint of something very sweet and even adorable makes perfect strangers feel like they've known you for years.

Features: Medium scale with substantial bone structure and facial bone and a curvy body type with soft facial features. Usually medium to slightly short (5'0"-5'6") with medium-short arms and legs and has broad bone structure. Hands and feet are medium-small and broad and/or fleshy. She is generally compact and curvy (more in and out than up and down) and she may be muscular. Generally becomes extremely fleshy and curvy in the hips and/or bust when overweight. Her facial bone structure (brow bone, nose, cheekbone, and jawline) may be broad and bluntly angular (wide with gently rolling topography) or soft (with relatively flat topography). Her facial features (eyes, lips) tend to be more round (circle or half circle) than linear (like parallel lines).

Celebrity Examples: Natalie Wood, Jennifer Lopez, Mila Kunis, Viola Davis, Emma Stone

Alternate variations: the Action Heroine, the Girl Next Door

Superpower: The Enchantress can warm any heart with her open, unaffected charm.

Kryptonite: Rigidity is contrary to her nature and gives us the feeling of a woman in a straight jacket.

Historical Periods: Regency, 1940's wartime, The late 1960's, The 1970s

What The Enchantress Wears Best

Shapes: The oval and the rounded square are the core shapes for the Enchantress. Bluntly angular shapes with softened edges, and open, rounded shapes repeat her innate design best.

Silhouette: The Enchantress' compact curves are best expressed through a relaxed fit-and-flare silhouette. Lines should be more in and out than vertical. She should avoid silhouettes that are straight with no waist or overly long.

Coordination style: An artistic mix-and-match approach conveys the casual nonchalance of the Enchantress best.

Fit & Fabrics: The Enchantress' garments should be relaxed, with plenty of drape and flow to allow for freedom of movement. The ideal fabrics for her are light and flowing or else chunky and textural.

Color: Colors that are flattering to her complexion should be mixed freely, as on a painters palette.

Motifs: Patterns and design details for the Enchantress should be delicate, rounded, organic and artistic. She may choose to pile it on or dress relatively simply, but minimalism is too controlled for her.

Tops: Necklines should be open and unconfined. Open V-necks, deep cowl necks, scoop necks, boat necks, asymmetrical, cross-over wraps and halters work well. Sleeves may have some drape and flow and armholes should be relaxed without being dropped too low.

Skirts: Either tube shapes with plenty of stretch or a full circle skirt. At minimum they should reach a couple of inches above the knee and at maximum they should be just below the knee.

Pants: Fitted skinny pants with a medium to high rise and no break.

Dresses: Flowing, relaxed fit and flare styles or body-skimming shapes in knit fabrics, especially wraps.

Jackets & Cardigans: Relaxed standard-length blazers with soft lapels and medium length, free-flowing draped cardigans with waist shaping.

Outerwear: Unstructured fit-and-flare coats with soft, asymmetrical collars.

Jewelry & Accessories: Delicate, artistic, and expressive. Unique pieces with an organic or hand-made quality.

Shoes: Substantial and soft-sided with tapered or rounded toes, or else open and bare. Moderately sized heels of medium thickness or flats.

Bags: Unstructured and neither too large nor too small. Textured materials and detailing and substantial hardware.

Hair: Softly layered hair that works with the natural texture is usually best. Very long hair works fine provided the texture can support it, otherwise mid-length with plenty of movement is best.

Makeup: Mostly natural in effect, with some soft and pretty effects like satin finish lips and eyeshadows and blushy cheeks. Very neutral, minimalist makeup can be used, providing the shades used are appropriate for your coloring.

Keywords: Medium-scale, softly angular, curve conscious, eclectic, organic, relaxed, sensual

The Sophisticate

Timeless and elegant, with a cleaner and sleeker twist that leans towards the here and now. There is a refined and reserved quality to you, you feel very balanced, like a fine wine. Your blend of moderate features with a subtle angularity feels tasteful and contemporary.

Features: Medium-large scale with slightly angular bone structure, slightly linear body type and moderate to slightly angular facial bones and features. Usually medium to slightly tall (5'3"-5'8") with medium-long arms and legs and medium width bone structure. Hands and feet are medium size and may be slightly broad or elongated. The sophisticate is generally lithe or slightly muscular, though like any type may be overweight, and if so excess flesh will gravitate to the lower body. Like all women she may have curves, but she tends to be more up and down than in and out. Her facial bone structure (brow bone, nose, cheekbone, and jawline) is moderate and well defined to slightly prominent and angular. Her facial features (eyes, lips) tend to be more linear (like parallel lines) than rounded (circle or half circle) or balanced between extremes. Her face appears calm and impassive when completely relaxed.

Celebrity Examples: Jacquie Kennedy, Gwyneth Paltrow, Vanessa Williams, Lucy Liu, Kate Middleton.

Alternate variations: the Fashion Editor, the CEO.

Superpower: The Sophisticate possesses an elegantly subtle strength. Like the perpetually chic tailored classics that flatter her, she doesn't need to shout to be heard.

Kryptonite: Frivolousness. Trivial notions negate the Sophisticate's unflappable practicality.

Historical Periods: Tailored classics from the 1950s and 60s.

What The Sophisticate Wears Best

Shapes: The golden rectangle and the square are the core shapes for the Sophisticate. Angular shapes with crisp edges repeat her innate design best.

Silhouette: Balanced proportions are key to accentuating the Sophisticate's symmetry. Lines should always be more vertical than horizontal. She should avoid silhouettes that are cropped, color blocked, or fit-and-flare.

Coordination style: Design elements should be tightly related and repetitive.

Fit & Fabrics: The Sophisticate's garments should sit slim to the body and be crisply tailored. The ideal fabrics for her are smooth, sleek, and structured.

Color: Colors should be coordinated and limited in number. Neutrals and subtle colors that flatter her coloring may make up the majority of her wardrobe, with the option to use a solitary accent color in any given outfit.

Motifs: Patterns and design details for the Sophisticate should be symmetrical, angular, edgy and modern. Allocation should be moderate, neither Spartan minimalism nor over the top embellishment.

Tops: Necklines should be subtly angular with clean edges. V-neck, Jewel neck, slot neck, cross-over and halter work well as do necklines that sweep upwards such as turtlenecks, mandarin collars, and man-tailored collars. Sleeves should be trim and crisp with high and tight armholes.

Skirts: Pencil skirts with a subtle taper or gentle A-Line skirts. Lengths should hover around the knee, not more than 2 inches above or below.

Pants: Straight and slim trouser-cut styles with a half break or slim cigarette with no break.

Dresses: Tailored columns or structured body-skimming shapes.

Jackets & Cardigans: Standard-length blazers with traditional or slightly sharpened lapels. Classic V-neck cardigans.

Outerwear: Well-fitted, tailored coats with the option for a slight edgy twist.

Jewelry & Accessories: Timeless, polished and substantial. Moderate in total amount.

Shoes: Elegantly tapered and streamlined or with a slightly sharp point. Heels neither kitten nor stiletto.

Bags: Structured, polished, solid and moderate in scale.

Hair: Simple and clean with minimal layers just for shaping. A subtle asymmetry can add interest. Medium to short lengths are best, depending on hair texture.

Makeup: A finished and well-manicured face with a very clean canvas and a good balance between features, neither overly soft nor overly graphic. Choose shades that are definitive but not ostentatious within the context of your coloring.

Keywords: Medium-scale, angular, elongated, balanced, coordinated, polished, tailored

The Princess

Always Lady-like, with a refined and elegant charm. Your moderate features convey elegance controlled sophistication, with an extra touch of soft, feminine grace. Every Princess, regardless of her history, personifies the idea of "to the manor born," and has an air of modern royalty.

Features: Medium-small scale with slightly delicate bone structure, subtle curves and soft facial features. Usually medium to slightly short (5'0"-5'6") with medium-short arms and legs and has moderate to slightly delicate bone structure. Hands and feet tend to be medium-small. The princess is generally compact and slightly curvy (slightly more in and out than up and down), though her hips may appear more exaggerated when overweight. Her facial bone structure (brow bone, nose, cheekbone, and jawline) is moderate and well defined to slightly rounded and flat. Her facial features (eyes, lips) tend to be more rounded (circle or half circle) than linear (like parallel lines) or balanced between extremes. Her face appears calm and impassive when completely relaxed.

Celebrity Examples: Grace Kelly, January Jones, Kerry Washington, Leighton Meester

Alternate variations: the Lady, the Heiress

Superpower: The Princess' refinement has a universal appeal that transcends time and space.

Kryptonite: Coarseness and vulgarity have no place next to this delicate woman.

Historical Periods: Tailored classics from the 1950s and 60s

What The Princess Wears Best

Shapes: The figure eight and the oval are the core shapes for the Princess. Rounded shapes with balanced proportions repeat her innate design best.

Silhouette: Balanced proportions are key to accentuating the Princess's symmetry. Lines should always be more fit-and-flare than vertical. She should avoid silhouettes that are overly long or large scale, color blocked, or straight up and down.

Coordination style: Design elements should be tightly related and repetitive.

Fit & Fabrics: The Princess's garments should sit close to the body and be softly tailored. The ideal fabrics for her are smooth and pliable but structured.

Color: Colors should be coordinated and limited in number. Neutrals and subtle colors that flatter her coloring may make up the majority of her wardrobe, with the option to use a solitary accent color in any given outfit.

Motifs: Patterns and design details for the Princess should be symmetrical, rounded, delicate and nostalgic. Allocation should be moderate, neither Spartan minimalism nor over the top embellishment.

Tops: Necklines should be subtly rounded with clean edges. Jewel neck, scoop neck, boat neck, secretary ties and subtle cowl necks work well as collared shirts provided they are not too sharp. Sleeves should be trim or have a slight drape with well-fitted high armholes.

Skirts: Pencil skirts with a subtle taper or full A-Lines and circle skirts. Lengths should hover around the knee, not more than 2 inches above or below.

Pants: Slim fitting and tapered to the ankle with no break.

Dresses: Tailored fit-and-flare styles or structured body-skimming shapes.

Jackets & Cardigans: Standard-length blazers with rounded edges and waist shaping or Chanel-style jackets. Classic jewel neck or shawl cardigans.

Outerwear: Well-fitted, tailored coats with fit-and-flare silhouettes.

Jewelry & Accessories: Timeless, polished and delicate. Moderate in total amount.

Shoes: Elegantly tapered or rounded through the toe. Heels neither kitten nor stiletto.

Bags: Structured, polished, lady-like and moderate in scale.

Hair: Simple and soft, layered only for shape with a soft edge or controlled wave or curl. Medium to slightly long is best depending on hair texture.

Makeup: A put-together and well defined face with a very polished skin finish and a bit of softness (well blended eye looks with a bit of shimmer, blushy cheeks, satin or slightly glossy lips). Shade selection should be classically feminine but not imperceptible, always in the context of your own coloring.

Keywords: Medium-scale, rounded, fit-and-flare, balanced, polished, tailored, coordinated

The Pixie

Spirited, unexpected, and playful with a penchant for pushing boundaries. Your mixture of opposites in physical features reminds us of unexpected juxtaposition in design, which in many cases represents the height of high fashion trendiness. Every Pixie, regardless of her age, personifies the idea of youthful exuberance, and has an air of playful rebelliousness.

Features: Medium-small scale with angular bone structure and facial bones, linear body type and soft facial features. Usually medium to extremely short (5'6" and under). Typically either narrow in bone structure with proportionately long arms and legs or broad in bone structure with short arms and legs. Hands and feet tend to be small and may be slightly wide. The pixie is generally lithe or slightly muscular, though like any type can be overweight and if so may appear deceptively curvy due to her compact frame. At normal weight, she is typically more up and down than in and out. Her facial bone structure (brow bone, nose, cheekbone, and jawline) is slightly sharp or bluntly angular (with some peaks and valleys in topography). Her facial features (eyes, lips) tend to be more rounded (circle or half circle) than linear (like parallel lines).

Celebrity Examples: Liza Minelli, Samira Wiley, Victoria Beckham, Zooey Deschanel, Lea Michelle.

Alternate variations: the Rebel, the Enfant Terrible, Peter Pan.

Superpower: The Pixie breaks rules and looks good doing it. Her wit and whimsy allow her to wear the most unexpected combinations to create something entirely new.

Kryptonite: Too much caution weighs the Pixie's wings down to the ground.

Historical Periods: 1920s flapper styles, 1960s mod, 1970s & 80s Punk

What The Pixie Wears Best

Shapes: The small equilateral triangle and the zigzag are the core shapes for the Pixie. Angular shapes with crisp edges mixed with some circles repeat her innate design best.

Silhouette: Abbreviated proportions are key to freeing the Pixie's lightness of being. Lines should be crisp and equal parts vertical and horizontal. She should avoid head to toe blocks of color and excessive fabric volume.

Coordination style: Design elements should be irregular and unexpected, and plentiful in total amount.

Fit & Fabrics: The Pixie's garments should sit slim to the body and be crisply tailored. The ideal fabrics for her are innovative, lightweight, and structured.

Color: Colors should be splashy, contrasting and as vibrant as the Pixie's coloring can handle. Neutrals should always be accented with color and atypical combinations of colors are excellent.

Motifs: Patterns and design details for the Pixie should be animated, angular, edgy and modern. Allocation should be plentiful, more is more.

Tops: Necklines should be angular with clean edges. V-neck, Jewel neck, slot neck, boat neck, small pointed collars and halter work well as do necklines that sweep upwards such as turtlenecks, mandarin collars, and stand collars. Sleeves should be trim and crisp with high and tight armholes.

Skirts: Pencil skirts with a subtle taper or gentle A-Line skirts. Skirts should be no longer than knee length and can be as mini as she likes.

Pants: Slim cigarette, cropped or with no break.

Dresses: Crisp A-Line shifts or structured body-skimming shapes.

Jackets & Cardigans: Cropped blazers with sharp lapels. Boxy, tailored cardigans with jacket styling.

Outerwear: Well-fitted, tailored coats or swing coats with plenty of design detail.

Jewelry & Accessories: Animated, irreverent, and flashy, using candy-like or unusual materials.

Shoes: Small and sharp or else chunky and playful.

Bags: Structured, graphic and moderate in scale.

Hair: Graphic shapes with some asymmetry. Regardless of texture, short (above the shoulder) or very short is always best.

Makeup: Crisp lines with clear edges (winged liner, cut creases, bold, opaque lips) suit best. Very exaggerated effect will be tolerated well, as will very colorful, shimmery or sparkly choices within the context of your personal coloring.

Keywords: Small-scale, angular, cropped, graphic, crisp, detailed, energetic

The Spitfire

Eternally girlish and ethereal, with an animated punch. There is a youthful and slightly mischievous quality to you, your energy sparkles and there always seems to be a twinkle in your eye. The inherent sweetness of your delicate small scale and rounded features is offset by a bit of angularity that adds a hyper-chic tailored crispness.

Features: Small scale with delicate bone structure and some curves, with angular facial bone structure and rounded features. Usually small to extremely short (5'5" and under). Typically delicate in bone structure with short arms and legs. Hands and feet tend to be small or extremely small and may be slightly wide. The spitfire is generally soft and slightly curvy, though like any type can be overweight and if so may appear deceptively fleshy due to her compact frame. At any weight she is more in and out than up and down. Her facial bone structure (brow bone, nose, cheekbone, and jawline) is generally flat and soft but may have some sharp angles (with some peaks and valleys in topography). Her facial features (eyes, lips) tend to be more rounded (circle or half circle) than linear (like parallel lines).

Celebrity Examples: Bette Davis, Nicki Minaj, Helena Bonham Carter, Anna Kendrick, Reese Witherspoon

Alternate variations: Tinkerbell, the Coquette

Superpower: The Spitfire's effervescent youthful energy explodes from her delicate person, filling any room she walks into.

Kryptonite: Heaviness buries the Spitfire's small form and snuffs her flame.

Historical Periods: 1920s flapper styles, 1960s mod

What The Spitfire Wears Best

Shapes: The petite circle and the scallop are the core shapes for the Spitfire. Rounded shapes with crisp edges mixed with some angles repeat her innate design best.

Silhouette: Abbreviated fit-and-flare proportions are key to freeing the Spitfire's lightness of being. Lines should be crisp and equal parts vertical and horizontal. She should avoid head to toe blocks of color and excessive fabric volume.

Coordination style: Design elements should be irregular and unexpected, and plentiful in total amount.

Fit & Fabrics: The Spitfire's garments should sit slim to the body and be fitted through the waist. The ideal fabrics for her are innovative, lightweight, and structured.

Color: Colors should be splashy, contrasting and as vibrant as the Spitfire's coloring can handle. Neutrals should always be accented with color and atypical combinations of colors are excellent.

Motifs: Patterns and design details for the Spitfire should be whimsical, rounded, and intricate. Allocation should be plentiful, more is more.

Tops: Necklines should be rounded with clean edges. Jewel neck, scoop neck, sweetheart, boat neck, small rounded collars and delicate straps work well. Sleeves should be trim and crisp with high and tight armholes.

Skirts: Pencil skirts tapered to the knee or full circle and poof shapes. Skirts should be no longer than knee length and can be as mini as she likes.

Pants: Slim skinny pants, tapered to the ankle, cropped or with no break.

Dresses: Crisply tailored fit and flare shapes or structured body-skimming shapes.

Jackets & Cardigans: Cropped blazers with soft lapels and waist shaping. Boxy, tailored cardigans with jacket styling.

Outerwear: Well-fitted, tailored fit and flare coats or swing coats with plenty of design detail.

Jewelry & Accessories: Animated, whimsical, and flashy, using candy-like or unusual materials.

Shoes: Small and delicate with tapered or rounded toes.

Bags: Small, structured, rounded, and graphic.

Hair: Chin-length or shorter with curl or rounded edges and small details like baby bangs or lots of tiny layers.

Makeup: Soft diffuse edges overall, with a bit of a graphic pop (as in liner, lips, etc). Very colorful, sparkly, or shimmery effects will be well tolerated within the confines of your personal coloring.

Keywords: Small-scale, rounded, curve conscious, crisp, detailed, graphic, energetic

The Femme Fatale

Delicately feminine, sexy, and glamorous, elevated with a high fashion edge. The feeling of a Femme Fatale is right out of the book of Old Hollywood Glamour. There is a magnetic and alluring quality to you, an ever-present flirtatious manner that others find irresistible. Added to this, is a slight thrill of danger that your added angularity brings. Extremely curvy and rounded physical features remind us of ornament in design, which in many cases represents the height of luxury - as in Marie Antoinette's Rococo or a Moroccan palace.

Features: Medium-small and curvy with delicate bone structure and mostly rounded features with some sharp features. Usually medium to extremely short (5'6" and under). Typically very delicate in bone structure with proportionate or slightly short arms and legs. Hands and feet tend to be small. The femme fatale is generally compact and extremely curvy with an exaggerated waist point but still somewhat small overall, though she tends to become extremely voluptuous when overweight. Her facial bone structure is generally delicate but sharply angular (with exaggerated peaks and valleys). Her facial features tend to be more rounded (circle or half circle) than linear (like parallel lines).

Celebrity Examples: Vivian Leigh, Diana Ross, Salma Hayek, Morena Baccarin, Jennifer Love Hewitt

Alternate variations: the Siren, the Courtesan, the Golden Age Starlet

Superpower: The Femme Fatale's magnetism is utterly arresting. Turning heads is what she was born for.

Kryptonite: Trying to fly under the radar. When she dresses inconspicuously, she succeeds all too well.

Historical Periods: the Victorian Era, the 1930s, 40s & 50s

What The Femme Fatale Wears best

Shapes: The oversize circle and the teardrop are the core shapes for the Femme Fatale. Rounded shapes that come to a point repeat her innate design best.

Silhouette: Exaggerated hourglass and fit-and-flare silhouettes that accentuate the waist. Lines should be curved and avoid straight vertical drops. She should avoid anything boxy or overly angular.

Coordination style: Design elements should be thematic but not repetitive, and plentiful in total amount.

Fit & Fabrics: The Femme Fatale's garments should hug the body and be fitted through the waist. The ideal fabrics for her are soft, fluid, and plush.

Color: Colors should be lush, like those of fruits and flowers (as pertains to her particular coloring) and used such that one flows into the next.

Motifs: Patterns and design details for the Femme Fatale should be luxurious, high-fashion, feminine and intricate. Allocation should be plentiful, particularly around the face.

Tops: Necklines should be open, rounded and soft, or else clean and sharp. Cowl neck, scoop neck, sweetheart, boat neck, off the shoulder and delicate straps work well as do necklines that move upwards such as jabots, mandarin collars, and keyhole turtlenecks. Sleeves should be trim to the wrist with high and tight armholes.

Skirts: Pencil skirts extremely tapered to the knee or full circle shapes. Skirts should be just above or just below the knee.

Pants: Slim skinny pants, tapered to the ankle, with no break.

Dresses: Lavish and sensual fit and flare shapes or fluid body-skimming shapes.

Jackets & Cardigans: Peplum blazers with soft lapels and very define waists. Cropped, waist emphasizing cardigans with open necklines.

Outerwear: Softly tailored fit and flare coats with angular details.

Jewelry & Accessories: Extremely ornate and glamorous with delicate construction and plenty of sparkle.

Shoes: Small and delicate with tapered or rounded toes and lots of embellishment.

Bags: Small, rounded and soft with delicate straps and hardware.

Hair: Long and ornately curled, or mid length with both curl and a bit of asymmetry.

Makeup: Very finished with exaggerated feminine details like extreme long lashes, shimmery or glittery eyes, overdrawn, glossy lips and very blushy cheeks. Some angled effects like winged liner may also be used. Shades should be feminine choices that flatter your personal coloring.

Keywords: Small-scale, delicately rounded, curve conscious, coordinated, embellished, theatrical

The Bombshell

Lushly feminine, soft, and sexy. There is a sweetly alluring quality to you, a head-to-toe softness that is absolutely enchanting. Bombshells are born exuding that effect every perfume ad promises.

Features: Medium-small and curvy with soft bone structure and rounded features. Usually medium to extremely short (5'6" and under). Typically small and slightly wide in bone structure with proportionate to short arms and legs. Hands and feet tend to be small. The bombshell is generally compact and extremely voluptuous with a small waist, though she becomes even more full when overweight. Her facial bone structure is generally soft and flat. Her facial features tend to be more rounded (circle or half circle) than linear (like parallel lines).

Celebrity Examples: Marilyn Monroe, Alyssa Milano, Amanda Seyfried, Kat Dennings, Paula Abdul

Alternate variations: the Southern Belle, the Calendar Girl

Superpower: The Bombshell's sensual sweetness has an enchanting nostalgic allure.

Kryptonite: The cutting edge. Anything harsh, severe or aggressively modern is dissonant against her backdrop of softness.

Historical Periods: the Romantic Era, the Rococo Era, 1940s & 50s

What The Bombshell Wears Best

Shapes: The circle is the core shape for the Bombshell. Rounded shapes with soft edges repeat her innate design best.

Silhouette: Soft hourglass and fit-and-flare silhouettes that accentuate the waist. Lines should be curved and avoid straight vertical drops. She should avoid anything boxy or overly angular.

Coordination style: Design elements should be thematic but not repetitive, and plentiful in total amount.

Fit & Fabrics: The Bombshell's garments should hug the body and be fitted through the waist. The ideal fabrics for her are soft, fluid, and plush.

Color: Colors should be lush, like those of fruits and flowers (as pertains to her particular coloring) and used such that one flows into the next.

Motifs: Patterns and design details for the Bombshell should be luscious, rounded, feminine and intricate. Allocation should be plentiful, particularly around the face.

Tops: Necklines should be open, rounded and soft. Cowl neck, scoop neck, sweetheart, off the shoulder and delicate straps work well. Sleeves may be fluid or trim to the wrist with fitted but not dropped armholes.

Skirts: Pencil skirts tapered to the knee, full circle or poof shapes. Skirts should be just above or just below the knee.

Pants: Slim skinny pants, fitted to the natural waist and tapered to the ankle, with no break.

Dresses: Lavish and sensual fit and flare shapes or fluid body-skimming shapes.

Jackets & Cardigans: Peplum blazers with soft lapels and very defined waists. Cropped, waist emphasizing cardigans with open necklines.

Outerwear: Softly draped fit and flare coats or swing coats.

Jewelry & Accessories: Soft, ornate and glamorous with delicate construction and plenty of sparkle.

Shoes: Small and delicate with rounded toes and lots of embellishment.

Bags: Rounded and soft with delicate straps and hardware.

Hair: As long as the hair texture will tolerate with very soft edges or lots of curl. Layers should be used only for shaping and softening.

Makeup: A finished face with classic "pinup" touches, or else a very skinlike base with extra soft, shimmery and glossy textures. Shades should be feminine choices consistent with your personal coloring.

Keywords: Medium-scale, lushly rounded, curve conscious, coordinated, embellished, sensual.

Now that you have discovered your Image Archetype, you have a sense of what it means to repeat your physical design in your style, as we talked about in Chapter 1. Using your physical design as a template for the clothing you choose will help you make better, more enhancing choices that create an ease to dressing that you may have never imagined was possible. In the next chapter, you will learn the final component of the discovery phase: your coloring.

Chapter 5
Know Your Colors

Color affects us emotionally perhaps more than any other design element in clothing. We have visceral, inexplicable reactions to it, and generally a very clear idea of which colors we believe to be for us or not. Unfortunately, color is, technically speaking rather inflexible. It behaves in accordance to predictable, scientific laws of color harmony and consequentially colors only either work for us or against us. In order to become the master of your appearance, you must learn to see color as a tool to accessing your complete visual potential rather than a preference.

The more levels of complexity you peel back when it comes to color theory, the deeper the onion seems to go. However, there are some basic tenets that are tremendously useful in determining which colors will work best for your natural coloring. First, colors with similar scientific dimensions look harmonious together, and those with opposing dimensions are dissonant. Color has three scientific dimensions, which are called Hue, Value, and Chroma. Every one of the 3-10 million colors we can see has a "setting" on each of these three dimensions that determines which colors it will harmonize with, including human skin tones.

Hue

The warmth or coolness of a color is described by its Hue. You may already know that orange is warmer than blue. This is true, however in human coloring, it's more important to understand that different variations of a "color" can be warmer or cooler, for example orange-reds are warmer than blue-reds.

Value

Value describes how light or dark a color is. If you imagine a grey scale with 10 steps leading gradually from white at the top to black at the bottom, those close to the top have high value and those at the bottom have low Value.

Chroma

Chroma is how bright or soft a color is. This is probably the most difficult dimension to understand, and sometimes it can be confused with Value, or even Hue. If you can imagine the pure hues of acrylic paints squeezed fresh out of the tube, what you are picturing is probably a fairly bright color – extremely pure and primary. Conversely, if you picture a work of art done in chalk pastels, those colors are probably fairly soft – dusty and grayish in tone.

This is important because the way that humans have evolved to see color is relative, not objective. What that means is that we see a myriad of visual illusions all the time to allow us to see what is *useful* and not necessarily what is *true*. One of the most powerful of these effects is called Simultaneous Contrast. Basically, whenever we see two colors next to each other (as for example, when your skin is next to a lipstick, blouse or hair color), they change each other's appearance, creating a distortion. You can see just how powerful the effect is in the diagram below.

What this example also teaches us is that we can't unsee these visual illusions just by knowing they are there. Even though you know the two clouds are the same shade, you still see a lighter one and a darker one. So even if your viewers were thinking "she looks sick today, but really it's just that chartreuse top", which seems unlikely, they would regardless still see the effect. Just as the right combinations of light and shadow can convince you that you are looking at two completely different shades of grey when they are in fact the same, simultaneous contrast can vastly change the subconscious perception of human faces. How old a woman seems to be, how well rested she seems to be, how healthy she seems to be, and even what mood she seems to be in can all be dramatically impacted by what color she has on, without us even knowing the illusion is there.

The solution to this problem is relatively simple, fortunately. Colors that have the same scientific dimensions as each other do not cause unflattering simultaneous contrast effects. The answer, as with all facets of your appearance, is to repeat your natural design. However, because these visual effects are in play, as well as a bevy of unhelpful stereotypes, you may not immediately be able to tell what your dimensions are, as my client Veronica learned.

I always know I'm in for a treat when a new client calls me three times and emails me twice before I can even get out of bed. Veronica was just the sort of client who, once she had decided she needed my help, needed it yesterday. As it happens, she had a big presentation for a major corporation on the horizon but I think she would have hunted me down until I saw her anyway. When she arrived at her appointment, I could see that she had incredible taste and a very high level of attention to detail. Every item she had on, from head to toe and from handbag to the very last pearl in her earrings had been chosen in accordance with a particular color palette, one which was cool-neutral, medium-dark, and very soft.

Unfortunately, as readily apparent to me as her already impeccable fashion sense was the thing she was missing, and doubtless, the reason she was in such a rush to see me. While Veronica had chosen colors that were beautiful together and very elegant they were a nightmare for her own coloring. Her skin looks splotchy and waxy, somehow both sallow and grey at the same time. Her eyes appeared dull and bleary, and an age spot on her cheek was so over-emphasized I wouldn't have been surprised if it introduced itself. The flat, single process blonde she was dying her hair to blend her smattering of grey looked lifeless and unrealistic.

Veronica thought she knew which colors suited her best, and yet something wasn't working that she couldn't put her finger on. And yet, I could see from the moment she walked in that this wasn't the real Veronica. As I walked her through the calculated fabric colors I use to make comparisons, she began to see things going in the opposite direction from what she expected. Having been blonde as a child with blue eyes, Veronica had assumed as many people do that her coloring must have been cool, soft and relatively light (or Summer, for those of you familiar with the seasonal coloring groups). She was able to discern for herself that an extremely light look overall didn't suit her, and so concluded that she must belong to the group in the Summer range that is slightly darker. This also happens to be the subgroup with the *softest* colors in that range.

What our analysis began to reveal from the very first drapes was that for her coloring, there was almost no such thing as too much brightness. Anything remotely bright lit up her laser blue eyes from within and gave her skin a clarity and glow as if she had just returned from a week at a spa, while soft colors drained the color from her face and made her look sick and tired. As shocked as she was, she saw it playing out right before her very eyes. She did indeed need colors that were cool-neutral and medium dark, but most importantly they had to be very bright, the opposite end of the Chroma dimension from what she had thought.

At the end of her appointment, when she pulled out the items she had thought were all wrong for her but couldn't give up and revealed a shiny satin blouse in the clearest blue-fuchsia and an elegant designer silk scarf in a delicate icy lemon yellow, all the pieces started to come together. She left wearing a lipstick in the same fuchsia as her blouse (that she wouldn't have dreamt of wearing a couple of hours before but could now see was a perfect extension of her natural coloring) and her own scarf with skin she could have paid a dermatologist thousands for – but she didn't need to, because she had it all along.

What Veronica learned was that despite her excellent eye she was no more objective about herself than anyone and that in addition she was under the grip of both some pretty powerful color illusions and a lifetime of ingrained misconceptions. She believed that she could "see" her own color dimensions, but no one can without a controlled comparison. She had fixed in her mind since childhood an image of herself as a towhead, when in fact in adulthood she had always been a light brunette. She thought that she could look up her coloring on a chart, but the truth is a person can have any combination of skin, hair and eye color and have any inherent color dimensions. Don't be fooled by color myths, they are usually generated by the garment and beauty industries to help some extra money leave your bank account. Choose colors that make you look healthy and alive, not because they're in this season or because they "work on everyone" (the only statement about color you can be 100% sure is false every time!).

If you find it hard to navigate the complexity of color on your own, I highly recommend a Personal Color Analysis from a certified 12 Blueprints analyst. What could take you years to navigate on your own can be determined in a couple of hours by a qualified professional. I provide this service myself for all of my clients and wouldn't dream of dressing someone to appear on camera without it.

In an ideal world, we would all look perfectly healthy, youthful, sophisticated, competent and approachable in whichever colors we preferred, but our eyes just don't see that way. Without even realizing it, your viewers make a split second decision about all these factors when they see you on screen and it greatly affects whether they keep watching long enough to want to work with you or click away. The success of your business is too important to let your fondness for mauve pinks stand in your way. There will always be an opportunity to buy a throw pillow or paint your toenails in colors you desire that may not be ideal for your image, but part of showing up as the face of your business means putting your client's experience first.

We are out of the discovery phase and ready to move into the implementation stage! In the next chapter, we will begin to combine your Image Archetype and personal coloring with your desires and goals to create an image that works for both you *and* your viewers.

Part Two:
Implementation

Chapter 6
Your Signature Style Manifesto

At this point, you already have all of the raw materials to craft your personal signature style. You know what goals you are trying to accomplish with your style, what you most deeply desire from your wardrobe, and what expresses your innate physical design. For many of my clients, this is the point at which they get stuck. In a sense, when a client reaches this point in their style journey they realize why they couldn't ever seem to get this done on their own – in short, it's complicated.

It's pretty obvious to me within minutes why the vast majority of my clients are sitting in my chair; however, Leah was one of those where I had to wonder a bit. Truthfully, she was innately stylish and had an effortless confidence that seemed to apply to her image as much as to her writing. Apart from what to me was a relatively minor adjustment in the colors she was wearing and validation on discarding some information from a previous stylist that she already concluded on her own wasn't serving her, it seemed like there wasn't a ton for me to teach her. Then we started to look into her goals and desires, and Leah's road block became clear. Leah absolutely loved the quiet chic of her cool, soft colors and the timeless-but-slightly-edgy elegance of her Sophisticate Image Archetype and easily saw herself in them. However, her work was for preteen girls who were more than a little precocious. It was important for Leah that she look like someone that girl would hope to be when she grows up, a mature adult, yes, but also one with a style that would be relatable for these girls. While I would normally never advise an adult woman to try to look cool to a bunch of teenagers, for Leah's business it was essential that she do so, albeit in an inherently adult way.

Already it was clear that Leah wasn't going to communicate to her audience effectively by looking like she just arrived from the Upper West Side. Her target client would just see her as one more rule-following adult who just wanted her to act her own age. Regardless, I could still see a vast array of options on how to craft Leah's style in a way that expressed her natural design and would speak to her target audience. It was Leah's desires that took her look from something still somewhat vague and amorphous to a laser focused, intentional signature style. Among her desires were the themes Badass (Moto jackets and ripped jeans) and Sexy (lace trims, cutouts, sheer tops over lingerie) as well as, paradoxically, Refined (designer goods of fine quality, impeccable tailoring) and Preppy (exactly what you'd think, prim, proper and very Old Money). While the parallels to her goals and her physical design were reasonably clear, there was also a certain *je-ne-sais-quoi,* an essential quality of Leah herself that was captured in her desires. Thus, we created a Signature Style for Leah that she brilliantly dubbed "Bad Girl Gone Good". The foundation of her look would consist of polished, high-quality hyper-traditional preppy pieces with unexpected accent pieces that were sourced directly from her badass & sexy themes. Her wardrobe would tell Leah's true story of being a sophisticated and successful woman who had built the life she wanted out of a rough background without ever losing her piss and vinegar. It would have been easy to see Leah's goals or desires as incompatible with her innate physicality. Instead, by laying out all the relevant factors from her goals, desires, and physicality and making creative connections between them, we constructed a unique signature style that works for her on all levels.

Identifying Your Signature Style

In order to combine your inputs from your desires, goals, and physicality most easily, I suggest collecting your abstract goals and desire work from Chapter 2 and 3 as well as your colors and Image Archetype from chapters 4 and 5 in front of you in tangible form. I highly recommend starting with the goals that will be most relevant to you as a public persona first and tackling the others later. As a general rule I prefer my clients to choose one overarching signature style, however two separate ones could be negotiated for professional and personal purposes if you keep them extremely compartmentalized, otherwise you will confuse yourself and make things too messy to work with.

The first step is to assemble your mind map. This is where we begin to lay out all of the work we have done so far. Start by writing key elements from each of your input sources (goals, desires, and physicality) on post-it notes of different colors and mount them on a board or wall where you can see them all. Choose a few key words from your goals exercise (I recommend 7-10) and write them on yellow sticky notes. Then, write a similar number of your themes and motifs from your desires exercise on pink notes, and the key words from your Image Archetype section and three color qualities (Hue, Value and Chroma settings from Chapter 5) on green notes. If you're more of a visual person or just have trouble describing visual elements in words, feel free to add pictures or whatever would be helpful for you to get the lay of the land. When I work with clients, we use an online version that is free for a single user at realtimeboard.com.

Once you have assembled your mind map, the next step is to notice where there may be overlap between your goals, desires, and physicality. Start by putting the most obvious matches (things that say the same word or very similar words) together into piles on your board. Next, start to connect the rest of the sticky notes by asking which words from your desires and your innate physicality can be used to accomplish your goals. When you find two that connect, move them into a pile together. There isn't always one right way of expressing your goals. For example, many of my clients have the goal of appearing "warm" (as in kind and caring) to their viewers, but some have chosen to express this kindness and caring through feminine touches, others through cozy and rustic fabrics, and still others through warm color temperatures. Anything that makes sense can work together, but

I doubt if you are going to express leadership through delicately ornate details. Look for the pattern that speaks to your goals in a language that is native to your physical design and appeases enough of your desires to feel right to the inner you. In the end you should probably have four to six piles representing the core concepts for your signature style.

It may be that you still have some elements that just don't seem to fit. This last step is where you have to make choices, remembering that there are only ever two to be made - integrate or move on. Let's say that one of your desired motifs is "all black everything" and yet your palette does not include black. This is the place to think about *why* black appeals to you so much. What does black say to you that is essential to who you are? There's no one answer here, I have had dozens of clients for whom black is a desired motif and it may be there for one client because it's practical, another because it's powerful, and another because it's timeless.

It may be black (or whatever motif or theme you are working with here) is all of those things to you, but it's most helpful to focus on one main reason. Then, consider whether that desire could be satisfied by something else on your board. Perhaps, for example, your desire to look powerful resonates with the boldness of your Queen Image Archetype and you can learn to express power through silhouette instead of color. For another client, the practicality of black might be just as easily found in charcoal grey shades that are more flattering.

In this step, you don't necessarily need to focus on only desire elements, though for many clients I find that is the core of the work to be done here. For example, you might, like my client

Tina who we met in Chapter 1, be a Pixie who wants to be seen as a paradigm shifter in her business and enjoys clothing that is sassy, playful and unique, but who has coloring that is somewhat light and pastel. In this case, we decided to focus on using the brightest colors in her palette as accents and on creating contrast by fully utilizing the darkest and lightest shades in her palette, which create the effect required by her goals, desires, and Image Archetype without compromising her complexion.

Though I typically advise my clients not to in this case, you can also just choose to wear the dissonant element and let something else fall off the board. One way of integrating your differing inputs is to simply release yourself from some of them, even if it compromises the aesthetic harmony of the result somewhat. If something is going to stop you from getting in front of the camera and hitting record, it may just not be worth worrying about. As the master of your own image, you get to make any decision you like, as long as you make it consciously and intentionally. Finally, instead of integrating you can choose to just acknowledge any elements you think you are ready to move on from and do so. These elements will always be either goals or desires, because we already know your innate physical self is going to be there for the rest of your life. Be sure to thank them for their service before you release them.

The creation of your mind map requires deep thought and can feel overwhelming. To help you, I've created a video that walks you through an example that you can find in my free toolkit at www.thefaceofthebusiness.com/toolkit.

Once you have created your core concept piles and reconciled any discrepancies on your board, you have finished your mind map the best way to prepare for the next step is to create a bulleted list of the technical elements of your signature style that will express your core concepts. Every good signature style has four main components:

1. Silhouette: line, shape, scale, proportion, fit, structure and balance.
2. Embellishment: pattern, design detail, texture and accessories
3. Color: hue, value, chroma, and specific shades
4. Coordination: how many of each type of design elements are used and how they are combined

Go through each of your core concepts and decide what silhouettes, embellishments, colors, and coordination must be used in order to satisfy each one, listing them as bullets as you go.

When you have gone through the design elements of your style, add a section to your bullet list called Concept and come up with a few words that describe how the style described in the detailed list feels and what is special about it. Finally, you have the option to add a section for very specific elements that you will be excited to wear 80-90% of the time, which I call Signature Elements. This might be a particular type of earring or a shade of pink, for example. It should be distinctive enough to be noticeable to others (so not your wedding band), but also not require too much effort to wear very consistently. Add these to your list as a finishing touch.

Let's check back in with my client Elise, who we met in Chapters 2 and 3. Elise's mind map combined her goals and desires with her Goddess Image Archetype and cool, dark and bright coloring. If you haven't already picked up my free toolkit, you can find a walkthrough of how we created Elise's mind map and categorized it into core concepts inside. Once we did that, Elise was able to use the core concepts on her mind map to create the following bulleted outline in preparation for writing her manifesto.

Silhouette
- Tailored, Crisp Edges
- Softly Sculptured; Well-Fitted, Curve-Conscious
- Large Scale
- Exotic Touches; Extreme/Unusual Shapes, Architectural
- Asymmetrical
- Elongated Lines

Embellishment
- Singular Powerful Statement
- Color Block/Graphic Contrasting
- Large Scale, Unique, Uncluttered
- Smooth, Luxurious Surface Textures

Color
- Black & White Contrast, All White, or All Black
- Jewel Tone, Saturated Color
- Silver or Icy Touches

Coordination
- Mixing Structured Things with Soft Sculpture; Bold/Dynamic with Feminine

- High Contrast or Bold Color
- One Powerful Statement Element or Elements tightly related
- 1 or 2 pieces of Statement Jewelry or Coordinating sets

Concept (what's great about it?)
- High-End, Stylized, and Meticulous
- Powerful, Commands Attention
- Exotic and Mysterious
- Dynamic and Dangerous

Signature Elements
- Dark hair in long, loose waves
- Large Statement Earrings or Necklace
- Black & White Contrast
- Bold lip: saturated color or Bold eye makeup: smoky eye or saturated base shade and/or liner

Creating Your Manifesto

Now that you've done the hard work, you get to do the fun part – create your Signature Style Manifesto. Using your bullet points, write a description (250-500 words, max) of all of the elements that remained once you integrated or eliminated all of them. I suggest starting with a paragraph that summarizes your concept using the concept section of your bullet list and being sure that it adequately summarizes the core concepts from your mind map. Many of my clients then go on to write a paragraph describing the way you will use each of the main categories from your bullet list: silhouette, embellishment, color and coordination. You can structure your manifesto however you like, just be sure that it includes all of the information from your bullet list. Some of my clients have even chosen to write their manifesto as a story! If it helps, you can describe your style in the third person, as you would a celebrity's personal style.

Do NOT finish your manifesto without including a plan for your hair and makeup. Whatever is going on from the waist up is the most important part of your style when it comes to being camera-ready. This doesn't mean you should neglect the bottom half of you – sooner or later it will matter, and you don't want to be filming a video distracted about how you hope no one lets on that you have pajama pants on just out of frame. However, the job of your clothing on-camera is to *tell the viewer where to look* and you want them to look at your face, and from there into your eyes. Make sure that your hair, makeup, jewelry, eyewear and necklines are allowing your viewers to get there in addition to working seamlessly with the overall concept of your Signature Style. Let's check back in with Elise and see how her bullets translate into her Manifesto.

The Prize Orchid juxtaposes structured, bold, and dynamic elements with those that are softly sculptured and feminine creating a total effect that is exotic, dangerous, meticulous and unmistakably powerful. She elevates high-end concepts by executing her style in a way that is well-fitted and purposeful. She is mysterious and unique, and incorporates bold elements that are distinctly "her" into her attire.

The Prize Orchid maintains a tailored silhouette that typically fits close to the body, composed of tightly related elements with elongated lines or a singular powerful statement, such as high contrast or a bold color. The large scale proportions and architectural and unusual shapes she employs ensure that she is always extraordinary. The fabrics in her wardrobe have smooth and luxurious surface textures. She wears a range of fabrics that are typically smooth (like ponte knit), plush (like fur), or sleek (like leather).

When the Prize Orchid wears embellishment, she tends to choose one major statement element that is unique and uncluttered. She most often chooses solids, but when she does choose patterns, they are large-scale and graphic, often employing black and white contrast. The design details she favors are edgy and alternative, such as spikes, studs, and zippers. To contrast these edgy and graphic elements, she mixes in soft draping to express her lushly feminine body shape. Like the rest of her embellishments, jewelry is either done as 1 or 2 statement pieces or as a coordinating set. Accessories in general tend to be kept to a minimum, however statement shoes and handbags are favorites.

Color for the Prize Orchid is used often in head-to-toe saturated jewel tones or as a pop of color against black and white. Otherwise, she sticks to all black or all white or the high contrast combination of both for the vast majority of her garments and accessories. She also uses metallic silver as an accent.

The Prize Orchid could be recognized anywhere by her long, dark hair which she always wears in either loose 40's style waves or pulled back from her face. Other signature elements she is almost never seen without are her bold lip color or bold eye makeup as well as black and white graphic contrast.

The final step to defining your Signature Style is to choose a name or defining statement. As you can see, we named Elise's

Manifesto The Prize Orchid. This name was chosen to reflect the meticulous care and the level of expertise she offers her clients, as well as the high drama inherent to her innate physicality and desires. Your manifesto name will be a useful litmus test later when you reach the action steps. For example, when Elise finds herself drawn to a boho maxi dress while shopping, she can ask herself whether that item aligns with "The Prize Orchid" (hint: probably not). For most items she doesn't even need to check it against her specific guidelines, so sticking to her manifesto becomes as easy as asking herself that one question when she's feeling unsure. Sometimes, a catchy title doesn't come to mind, and in that case you can get the same effect out of a statement, such as "I am relaxed, modern, graphic, and colorful."

In order to help give you the general idea of what should go in your manifesto, I've included a library of client manifestos along with examples of how they used them in their wardrobes, as well as some prompts to inspire your manifesto name in my free toolkit. You can check them out at www.thefaceofthebusiness.com/toolkit.

That's it! You've completed the insight portion of this book and created a clear vision of the camera-ready woman of style you are going to become. Of course, all that effort will be wasted if you stop here and leave your manifesto to collect dust. Treat yourself to a glass of wine, a chocolate croissant, or a mani-pedi (or heck, all three) and read on to bring your vision to life.

Chapter 1
Wardrobe

Much as you may purchase items that align with the Signature Style you just created, you will not get the result until you reconcile your new vision of yourself with the contents of your closet. No matter how much of a tight ship you think you've been running when it comes to clean outs, ghosts of versions of you that are no longer or never were are undoubtedly lurking in there. That said, I believe in a somewhat gradual multi-step process for anyone who doesn't have the cash to burn it all and start over. Which, by the way if you do, you might seriously consider. Either way, there will likely be some resistance to tackle and following the process I outline in this chapter will help you overcome it where it matters most.

Try to do this when you have access to as much of your wardrobe as possible, which means not in the laundry or at the cleaner or in storage. Your new wardrobe will make much more sense so you won't have to have every single thing laundered to make an outfit but for now you want to be able to go through every last piece. I suggest some loose organization by category before you get started, but for the first pass it's not a must.

The First Pass

The very first thing you must do is to get rid of anything that has no hope of being of use in bringing your signature style to life. This includes any items which are irreparably worn or damaged, obviously outdated, or that you just hate wearing for any reason (no matter how perfect it may seem on paper). You don't ever want to send your viewers the message that you don't care enough to take care of yourself, or that you are no longer relevant, or that you're just uncomfortable for an unspecified reason that they will undoubtedly interpret in the least positive light. Oh, and one more thing – get rid of anything that does not fit you right now, as in today. The woman who has mastered her image does not wait to lose the weight to get it done. Be that woman now and accept that the day when you fit into these items may not come anytime soon or ever. And yes, that includes items that are too big, as my client Tonya learned.

I've been in a lot of wardrobes, from almost incomprehensibly lean ones to those 25 years past due for a clean out. Never have I seen the likes of Tonya's wardrobe. By the time she asked me to come and look at it, we had already worked together for some time, and Tonya had a pretty good handle on how to choose new items that worked for her, but I sensed repeatedly that there was some roadblock hanging around that we hadn't quite broken through. She had, as it happened, lost a little bit of weight and felt that it would be a good time to go through things. When I arrived, I was greeted by at least half a dozen giant Rubbermaid containers full of clothing, which was only supplemental to multiple closets and a large chest. One would think that with all these clothes there would be an almost limitless selection of styles, but to my dismay a solid quarter of this storage was dedicated to black trousers and jeans in at least 3 different sizes, probably close to 100 pairs of just these two item types. Tonya had experienced a lot of weight fluctuations in the past few years prior and at each stage she had hung onto the other sizes she had oscillated between. Without realizing it, Tonya was willing herself to continue this cycle by keeping these alternates around. When you recreate yourself but leave your old clothes hanging around indefinitely, you are secretly keeping a part of the old you alive, which prevents you from actually moving on. Tonya needed to rip the band-aid off. While we got rid of other things that day based on other criteria, the main focus was on whittling down to those items she could wear in the here and now.

Aligning with Your Manifesto

Once you have completed this first pass, your wardrobe may be feeling a lot lighter and more manageable (possibly even a bit anemic) but you aren't finished just yet. Now that all of the items remaining can actually be worn, you can start to evaluate them on the basis of how well they align with your

Signature Style Manifesto. Go through each piece and identify it as category A, B or C.

Category A consists only of those items that align perfectly with your Signature Style Manifesto in every way. Guess what, you may have absolutely nothing in this category! That is completely fine because the likelihood is that your wardrobe will never fit 100% into this category and that is totally normal. Your Signature Style Manifesto describes an idealized version of your wardrobe and we are living in the real world where compromises must sometimes be made. That doesn't even remotely mean that you will not become a camera-ready woman of style- in fact allocating compromises wisely is a key skill of the woman who has mastered her image. Dedicate an area of your closet to these items to the extent that you do own them so that they are easily accessible.

Category B consists of any items which do align with some part of your Signature Style Manifesto but aren't perfect. If you are like most of my clients (including myself) you will always have some part of your wardrobe in category B. For instance, you may have a dress that you totally love which is the perfect style to express your Image Archetype, sends the exact right message to your ideal viewers, looks great on camera and fits like a glove, but is a slightly sub-par color. It may seem obvious that you should keep and wear this item, but many of my clients use these minor flaws as an excuse not to ever let the vision they crafted in their manifesto see the light of day. Do beware of turning category B into a rationalization zone. It can be a steep, slippery slope between accepting that your wardrobe doesn't need to be comprised of only perfect items and going back to filling it with whatever catches your eye. As a rule of thumb, you should probably accept only one element that is a departure from your manifesto per item, possibly two if the item is indispensable practically. Many women have enough in these first two categories to dress them for most occasions. However, if you don't, no need to panic.

Category C will be essentially everything that remains after removing the unwearable items from the first pass and the items that work well for you. I have grouped them together instead of separating the categories out further because they all have one thing in common – sooner or later, you will want to get rid of them. There are, however, three different kinds of items in the category - items you want to keep but shouldn't, items you want to get rid of and should, and items you want to get rid of but can't. It should probably be abundantly obvious what to do with the things you want to get rid of and should. Make haste and schedule the goodwill pickup. Some of my clients like to try to resell things, which is fine so long as you are the type to get it done quickly and you don't expect to get much value back out of them. Don't let it become a roadblock when bags of things you don't even vaguely want are hanging around for months on end.

As for the items that you know you should get rid of but for one reason or another have an attachment to, I suggest that you pack these things up but don't get rid of them. No, not forever. You are going to set a calendar reminder for 6 months from now, during which period you will be on a little holiday from these items, dipping your toes into the refreshing waters of your new Signature Style. Put them somewhere difficult to access so that you have to really want to wear them to take them out and don't end up just pulling them out of a box on your closet floor on laundry day. Trying to get rid of things you truly do not want to get rid of right now will only create reactionary resistance, giving you the impression that some outside force is in fact in control of your wardrobe instead of you. It also creates unnecessarily high stakes to testing out your Signature Style. Give yourself this opportunity to explore safely. Usually, at the end of this holiday my clients are able to get rid of most of the items they put away with no emotional trauma. You will have had time to become the version of yourself that you envisioned in your manifesto that will then be a better reward than keeping the items you put away. If there are things you still wish to keep, consider whether they may be something that actually can work for your signature style. Your proficiency and sophistication level as the master of your own image will improve rapidly and you may have a new perspective on some of these items after a few months.

Finally, we come to those items that you don't actually want to keep but won't be able to get dressed without. For example, maybe you have a pair of pants in an unflattering cut that you simply can't get dressed to meet clients without just now. For now, keep these things. However, these will be the first items on the list of things you will be looking to purchase as we move towards shopping in the next chapter. If you don't make a list of what you need, you will end up doing two things – purchasing too much of certain things, and never purchasing others. Generally, the things in your wardrobe that you are really unhappy with but can't get dressed without are item types you avoid buying. Come up with an ideal replacement for each item in this category based on your Signature Style Manifesto and start a running list with these items up top.

As an optional extra step, once you have completed your cleanout you can upload the items remaining in your active wardrobe (A and B items and C items you can't dress without) to the Stylebook app. I will warn you, the initial workload in getting a relatively large number of items uploaded at once is significant. However, once you do you have access to a great number of tools that will be very helpful in getting a firm idea of what you currently have versus what you need and also in going forward to shopping and creating outfits. I request that all of my clients use this tool so that they can have the information they need for success in implementing their Manifesto at their fingertips.

Looking for Gaps

Once you have a list of the items that need emergency replacement, you can revisit categories A and B and compare them to your manifesto looking for gaps that need to be filled in. Maybe your manifesto states that blazers are a signature item for you and that you will wear them in all of your videos, but you only have one that meets either category A or B criteria. Maybe your manifesto states that you will always wear big, sparkly earrings on camera, but you don't actually have any. Add these items to the list along with the items that need replacement. You don't need to try to replace category B items, but you do want to aim to acquire new things that meet the criteria for category A.

Finally, in a second column, create a short list of things you have way more of than you need in categories A and B. Tonya isn't the only one who unconsciously buys a certain item type or two over and over and over. Nearly all of my clients have at least one item that is a favorite to shop for and that they will continually buy, draining time, resources, and wardrobe space from other essentials if they aren't careful. Mine are earrings and special occasion dresses (what can I say, I love sparkly shit and taffeta). Write them down next to the list of things you do need to remind yourself while you're shopping that you don't need to buy any more of those things just now and redirect your attention to a more productive area of the store. Speaking of which, grab that list, put on some comfortable shoes and follow me to a whole new approach to shopping.

Chapter 8
Shopping

You, like most of my clients, have been shopping for, purchasing and wearing clothing for your entire adult life. And yet, the majority of my clients look upon shopping as some great mystery of the universe – basically, they're not even sure what being good at it would mean but they're pretty confident that whatever shopping skills are, they don't have them. As women it can be tough to admit that we weren't just born with expertise in all aesthetic realms, but the truth is it's a learned skill like anything else, and not necessarily one you can acquire on your own. Rest assured that if you feel you've been failing at shopping so far, you're about to learn a very different approach.

The garment and beauty industries don't want you to be good at shopping. Good shoppers demand more for their money and they make fewer mistakes, which means they spend less. It's in the interest of these industries to perpetuate ideas about shopping that prevent you from ever getting good at it. You've almost undoubtedly heard these over and over, and they sound innocent "This looks good on everyone." "You should buy this it's *so* on-trend." "Let's just brighten you up with some red lipstick and highlights." "As long as you love it, you're sure to look great in it!"

Don't be fooled. These messages are only perpetuated to part you from your money. You are the one who is going to have to deal with the fallout, not the smiling and lovely girl in the shop who is assuring you that skirt you're sure is too short looks just fine. (In fact you just did last chapter – fun, eh?) There's basically no avoiding the industry unless you want to leave your house naked with no makeup, so you are going to need to develop a strategy to make it work for you and to develop the confidence to tune out marketing that doesn't serve you. By flipping the relationship between yourself and the garment industry from one in which you live up to their expectations to one in which they are expected to cater to you, you will take back authority and become the master of your own image, as my client Helen did.

I first met Helen when she decided to hop on a plane and come to Philadelphia to see me before a photo shoot for her website. Evidently she had been following me on social media for some time and thought that she'd best just cut to the chase and come right to me to get her look sorted out. If there's one thing that motivates my clients to bite the bullet and work with me more than anything else, it's a major upcoming event that they have nothing to wear for (more on that later). I could have typed Helen as a Bombshell from a mile away. Her bodacious curves and petite stature along with her effervescent, charmingly flirtatious personality just screamed Marilyn Monroe reincarnated. In Helen's case, none of this information was especially surprising, so the real transformation didn't happen for her until we hit the shops.

When I shop with my clients, I pull TONS of things for them at a time. I always like to leave room for serendipity so I will include something in our pile even if I think it's a long shot. And in Helen's case, we rejected probably 80% of it. About halfway through our first day of shopping, I could tell something was bugging her. We broke for lunch and I asked her what was going on.

As it turned out, she was concerned that we weren't finding enough. She felt that the amount of things we rejected were somehow a reflection on her, a feeling that felt eerily familiar from shopping trips with friends throughout her life. I calmly reassured her that there was nothing wrong with her or the shopping we had done that day. I explained that most women are just not as voluptuously curvy as she is, and ready-to-wear clothing is targeted at the average consumer. Any consumer who has an element of their physicality that sits at an extreme end of the bell curve will experience a similar phenomenon – *there is less in stores for them.* There's no reason to assume that any store you walk into will necessarily have even one thing that is worth bringing home. Fortunately, we live in a world where the limitless choices of garments means that even those who do not sit in the middle of the bell curve have plenty of choices, just not as many.

Suddenly, Helen perked up. She was actually excited that she finally had an explanation for why she so frequently went shopping with a girlfriend and came home empty-handed while her friend made several purchases, or worse, bought things she thought were cute on the hanger but never ended up wearing. She wasn't too fussy and there was nothing wrong with her body shape. Releasing herself from the need to always buy something when she went shopping meant that Helen was able to stop buying things that didn't necessarily suit her just to feel like she was accomplishing something. She began to see potential purchases as needing to work for her, not the other way around. We finished the day having found more than enough that truly suited her, and she now has one of the most carefully selected closets of any client I have ever worked with.

When to Shop

From now on, shopping is neither a fun hobby nor something you do at the last minute when you absolutely have to. When you are acquiring new pieces for your wardrobe, you should do it with intention and a plan, just as you would in any other aspect of your business. We have already created your Signature Style Manifesto and a list of pieces your wardrobe is missing. The next step is to decide where to look for those pieces and by when you need to have them.

Depending on how soon you will need to be prepared for some of the occasions you listed in chapter 1 and how much was already in your wardrobe that aligned with your manifesto, you may be under more or less of a time crunch. This is important because it will give you an idea of how much you need to spend to get the job done. Of course, we aren't talking about spending enough to get passable quality. I'll presume you know that clothing targeted to women who are "perpetually 21" is not appropriate attire for the face of your business.

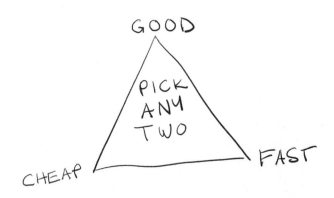

When it comes to shopping for clothing, I find the above adage to be true. Too many of my clients who always shop under pressure and have a very finite limit on what they want to spend end up with a wardrobe that just frankly, sucks, typically in the sense that it is painfully boring or poor quality or both. That leaves only two options – you either allow yourself to shop under pressure and spend very liberally to get what you want, or you can take your time and plan things out in advance and get an amazing wardrobe very affordably.

I'm not of the opinion that one of these strategies is inherently better than the other and I have been known to employ them both for both my clients and myself. I do think that you should be aware of which one you are choosing to avoid either getting locked into the good-fast-expensive strategy or falling prey to making purchases quickly and cheaply. Don't wait until the weekend before you shoot the video for your new course to find something to wear unless you are prepared to spend all weekend and however much money it takes to get outfits together that align with your Signature Style Manifesto. Since you already have a list of goals that includes your needs for a wide variety of occasions, you can decide now whether you are going to shop in advance or at the last minute for each of those occasions. I do encourage you to take the slow-cheap-good route for both everyday occasions and anything that involves being photographed or videotaped for your business. Relying on spending a bundle of cash to tide you through these situations will work, but it also can add a lot of stress and panic around getting dressed that you just don't need taking your attention away from more important things.

Where to Shop

As a final step, you should give some thought to where you will shop. Choosing the right stores for you may take some trial and error at first, but it will save you hours of fruitless searching in the long run. Usually before working with me my clients shop at a very limited number of retailers mainly chosen because they are convenient or because they appeal to their desires, and then later because it simply becomes habit to shop at those places. Reevaluate your favorite shopping destinations in light of your Signature Style Manifesto. Do they carry the kind of things the women described in your manifesto would wear? If your Signature Style is called "the Italian fashion editor" you probably aren't going to have much success at Anthropologie, regardless of how much of a fun and pretty place it may be to shop. Following the breadcrumbs from items that look perfect for you on Pinterest or polyvore can lead you to discover new sources you may never have heard of.

Another dimension to this equation is whether to shop in person or online. They both have their benefits, but I will go ahead and confess I think shopping online is far more effective in general. It may be that you live in an area with amazing shops and can easily find things in person, however, and there are other more ephemeral benefits to shopping in stores, such as having a clearer idea of what the products actually are and of course the convenience of being able to try things *before* purchasing them. Still, the vast array of options and superior ability to sort through them online makes it hard to compare the two.

Speaking of being able to sort through options, one of my very favorite and most used tools is shopstyle.com. It's totally free and you don't even need to sign up. I have used a lot of shopping search engines, but I get the best results on this one. I won't say it always finds what I need if it is out there, and it's worth noting that for plus, petite, or tall its performance is significantly worse. However, it can save you loads of time when you are looking for something very specific, like a chocolate brown camisole or a printed chiffon blouse, which you can just type right into the search bar on the site. You can add filters for loads of factors, including, size, price, color, etc. to avoid wasting time sifting through items that won't work for you anyway. This can be a tremendous resource in filling in the gaps you identified in the last chapter. I've included a video tutorial in my free toolkit, which you can find at www.thefaceofthebusiness.com/toolkit.

If you are going to shop online, it's important to decide ahead of time that you aren't purchasing things, you are trying them on, and the shipping fees to the extent they are charged are a convenience charge for the service of being able to try on almost any garment that exists without having to commit to purchasing it. *Never* order things on final sale (regular sales that involve being able to make returns are great!). The woman who masters her image doesn't compromise it for discounts, no matter how deep.

Establishing a Benchmark

The single most important skill you can develop as a shopper is knowing when something is working for you and when it is not. You have created a road map in the form of your Signature Style Manifesto to help you choose things that do work, but there will still be plenty of times when what should work on paper just doesn't. On the other hand, every single week one of my clients asks me why something isn't working when in fact, it looks fabulous. Why don't they know? My clients don't realize it, but they are actually comparing how they look in that particular garment to *how someone else would look.* And let me spoil it for you, that someone else they are imagining has a different body that doesn't do whatever they wish theirs wasn't doing.

The dressing room (or the metaphorical one at home in your bathroom when something new has arrived in the mail) may as well be a special shrine where women go to worship their idea of the ideal body and to inwardly punish themselves for not having it. (And by the way, there's a 99.9% chance that this is the main reason you hate shopping.) It can take time and practice to get out of the habit of making the act of trying on clothing into a body-shaming ritual for one. In order to start to come up for air, you will need to commit to making comparisons only to yourself. This can be hard to do in the abstract, so I use a tool I call a benchmark to help my clients hold onto that objective. Basically, a benchmark is a photo of you in the best look that you currently own. I identify this look for my clients, but you can easily do it on your own.

It may be that you are not very good at deciding whether something looks good or bad even when it's right in front of you. Something you are much better at is telling which is better between two options that you can see side by side. We all have an inherent and surprisingly objective sense of beauty. This is why you can hear a wrong note on the piano even if you know nothing about how music should be put together or even which notes are being played. You can tap into your innate sense of beauty by using comparison as a tool. Try on some outfits from the A and B categories of your wardrobe that are as close to alignment with your Signature Style Manifesto as possible. It may be that you already have an idea of one or two things that you feel really great in, and totally understand why after crafting your manifesto. Take a full-length picture of each. When you are done, load them up on your computer screen so that you can see small thumbnails of each one side by side. Which one are you naturally drawn to? If you met these women at a party, which one would you be most interested to talk to? In which photo do you see no discrepancy between the woman and her clothing? Which woman would you buy from?

Don't worry if you can't help but feel that you look awful in all of the photos. There is nothing productive about feeling bad for feeling bad. Culturally, we are very deconditioned from seeing pictures of women with physical features outside of a very narrow range who have been carefully posed and retouched. Allow that thought and don't argue with it, and then proceed with answering the questions above. As we discussed in prior chapters, it's important that you avoid asking someone else. Unless they are an image expert, they can't help you, much as they may want to or believe they can because they lack both a relevant knowledge base and your life experience. Your gut instinct reaction from the split second you opened the photos is probably the right answer.

Once you have established your benchmark, be sure to keep that photo on your phone or in your purse while you shop. Each time you are considering a purchase, go ahead and snap a picture and compare between the new outfit with your baseline. Ideally, you want the new items you bring into your wardrobe to be at least as effective on you as your baseline or better. Don't limit this tool to just clothing, it works perfectly with hairstyles, makeup, and even accessories. Even different handbags will lay against your body differently, so you can use comparison to make the best decision. Not only does this ensure that you will continue moving forward towards mastering your image instead of backsliding, but it will also train you over time to stop comparing yourself to an imaginary ideal you can never measure up to and instead focus on using your style to create the best possible version of you.

Finding the Magic

Most people have one or two basic silhouettes that work the best for them, and you will be able to discover them fairly easily by using your benchmark. In fact, you may quickly start to notice best lipsticks, color combinations, shoe shapes, and etc. While knowing what works for you is hugely empowering when it comes to shopping, what may happen over time is that you start to get tunnel vision and choose a few garment types over and over. That can work fine as a strategy, but it is also somewhat limiting to your own ever-expanding idea of your full visual potential. I absolutely advocate to sticking with what you know works on your body for 80% of your wardrobe at least. However, I also suggest that when you go shopping, about 20% of the things you try should be items that you are unsure about but intrigued by, and that you feel would represent your Signature Style Manifesto, even if in a slightly different way than usual. That doesn't mean that you will end up purchasing these things, as they may after all not work (which will only more fully flesh out your self-awareness of what works for you). Those that you do keep, however, can be that extra sprinkling of fairy dust on your style that makes others wonder "How on Earth did she know to do that?"

This technique is optional, and if your wardrobe needs a ton of work at the beginning, you may want to forgo it until you have a solid base of pieces. A wardrobe that always delivers the same thing and is a little one note is far preferable to one that makes no sense with itself or with the person wearing it.

Learning how to shop with intention and control the inputs into your wardrobe is a critical step to mastering your image. While employing the techniques above will admittedly make shopping more difficult, it will make *dressing* much easier. Of the two, dressing is the one that you will do every single day, and the one that will directly affect whether others see you as the master of your own image or not. Shopping is a supporting activity that you do far less frequently.

Chapter 9
Crafting Outfits

Your signature style is almost ready for it's big debut on screen! All the raw materials needed to leverage your appearance in your business are hanging in your closet. There's just one last thing to do, which is to put all the pieces together. It is in fact possible to create an incredible Signature Style Manifesto and a wardrobe of very excellent clothes that are independently very well suited to you and still not be able to get dressed.

The most common pattern I notice is that clients accidentally make outfits out of all solid, neutral colored basics and skip the accessories. These outfits are technically "correct" in that they fit with the client's Signature Style Manifesto and don't distort the client's physical features, but they just fall flat. This is one of the sneakiest ways you can try to stay hidden and prove to yourselves that you are not, in fact, a camera-ready women of style. In order to step up and reach the person who needs your message the most, you are going to have to wear something that someone out there could disapprove of.

For my client Romy, this was her most major setback. Romy is a very exotic looking Spitfire with highly contrasting, cool coloring under 5' tall who had always dressed in very typical (admittedly very expensive and high quality) professional attire before we met. She understood completely my recommendations to inject energy and play into her clothes to take advantage of her youthful effervescence and to wear saturated lip color that would give the most life to her complexion.

And yet, for months I would get a call... yet again she had filmed a video and didn't like how she looked! And each time when I saw what she had on, I didn't wonder why. While intellectually she knew what was best for her, she kept going back to plain jane basics and beige lipstick. Her story was that she just liked those things, but after doing her desire board that contained themes like "striking" and "iconic," I wasn't buying it. What was really going on beneath the surface was that she actually longed to look unique and distinctive, but was afraid of the comments about what she was wearing.

After all, almost anything could offend someone. The very design elements that my clients avoid or fear wearing are the ones that will have the most power to express their visual potential. Generally these include, color, prints, texture, design details and accessories. If you create outfits that don't include any of these design elements, they will be almost guaranteed to look lazy and bland and they will not inspire anyone to click the subscribe button. Think of the worst thing someone could possibly say about you for wearing a particular print or a color. Is it so bad that it's worth keeping yourself and your business small? Probably not. If you have been dressing extremely plainly, you can start small by incorporating just two of the five elements listed above. Even if you are not very advanced at outfit creation, this should make it fairly easy to put something together that says enough to avoid saying nothing at all.

On the other hand, I do have a small subset of clients who want to wear too much all at once. I appreciate their enthusiasm! However, too many design elements screaming at the top of their lungs for attention can be hard to process and consequentially we fail to get the impact of even one of their super cool garments. How quickly this happens will differ depending on your Image Archetype, so be sure to check back over that section if you are struggling to find the line.

My client Lily struggled with this one. When I first met Lily, she was sure she was a Pixie, but in fact her Image Archetype was the Enchantress. I soon realized that her attraction to the Pixie type had a lot to do with her fondness for garments with a lot going on. She regularly mixed very detail heavy items but unfortunately they often didn't work with her or each other, which resulted in awkward and unprofessional photos and videos. When I advised her to buy basics to mix in with statement pieces, she said "Well surely even basics must have some unique detail..." Digging into that, I discovered her problem was almost the opposite of Romy's – Lily was afraid that she would look boring and that her videos would be lost in a sea of others on the same topic. Her desperation to stand out was just the manifestation of her fear that she didn't have anything unique or special to offer. Once she acknowledged that, we were able to craft outfits that were plenty interesting enough to be effective and also flattering and tasteful.

A Formula for Fascinating Outfits

To be totally honest, I always create outfits by feel, but some of my clients find it useful to have a formula. For most people, the formula of one or two basics, one statement piece (something with enough interest to be the focal point), one finishing piece (a cardigan, jacket or optional accessory) and basic accessories works well. So a Muse with the signature style Exotic Urban Chic might wear a loose fitting V-neck t-shirt half-tucked into high waisted jeans (basics) with a patterned fringe-y kimono (statement), a wide tooled leather belt (finisher), and a pair of hoops, a pendant on a long chain, strappy sandals, and a slouchy hobo (accessories). A Princess with the Signature Style Manifesto Understated French Glamour might wear a well-fitted scoop neck t-shirt with solid wash, straight leg jeans (basics) with a watercolor butterfly print silk scarf (statement), a cashmere cardigan with silk trim (finisher), a pair of studs, a tennis bracelet, a watch, and ballet flats (accessories).

When crafting outfits, it will be especially important to refer back to the work you did in Chapter 2 on your goals. This will both give you an idea of how many outfits you need for what types of occasions and also remind you to craft your outfits with your ideal audience in mind. For most occasions, the main point will be to create the right nuance within the bounds of your

Signature Style Manifesto. For example, an Enchantress with the signature style Sensual Bohemian who is a weight loss coach will want to lean more towards expressing the artistic, intuitive and soft side of her signature style for intimate client meetings rather than leaning too heavily on overt sex appeal, which may well be a part of her style for other occasions. On the other hand, maybe she leads retreats in Rio where her clients learn to enjoy their bodies, which would be the perfect time for her to show some skin. Remember to ask yourself who your target audience needs you to be in order to serve them. Your Signature Style Manifesto was written with your goals in mind, so honing in on the perfect outfit for each scenario should be seamless.

Pitfalls for On-Camera Outfits

For video specifically, there are some particular pitfalls to be avoided due to the way certain things get interpreted by a camera. First of all, if you are not in control of the camera and lighting (as in television appearances for example) always be sure to ask when booking the appearance if they have any guidelines as far as what they would like you to wear. Even so, bring at least one back-up option in case the production team feels they can't work with what you have on. If you are filming yourself, do outfit tests on camera and watch the footage back before filming 10 videos that may turn out to be unusable.

In terms of color, large, solid blocks of pure white or black can be difficult for video, because they dramatically affect the way the camera interprets the lighting condition in the room. Very bright red colors in large blocks can also have strange effects on camera. Smaller blocks or accents of these colors are usually fine. Patterns can look great on camera, but certain types of patterns that are too small, such as pinstripes, checks or herringbones, can cause a distracting vibrating distortion of the picture. Very sparkly things can also be an issue because the reflection can become very "hot" under the lights, meaning that area of the screen will show up as white or very bright and light. I have even had certain buttons reflect light like crazy on set, yet another reason to plan ahead and always have a back up choice.

Certain glasses lenses can also create this effect, so if you will wear them on camera and don't already have good glare-reducing lenses, investing in some is a priority. Likewise, jewelry or fabrics that make noise can be picked up by your mic, which is usually a bad thing unless it's a choreographed element of your video. Fit issues that aren't especially apparent in person can also really show up on camera, so when you are doing your tests be sure to notice how your garments are laying. You can almost always get away with using pins to adjust things where they won't be seen as long as you are aware of the issue ahead of time.

I would highly, highly suggest that you never go on camera without makeup on. Likewise for wash and wear hair in most cases (the exception being if it's extremely short). It's possible that for things like Skype meetings with clients or Facebook live videos or Periscopes, not wearing makeup or doing any hair styling may be an aspect of your signature style, but for anything more formal, it's really not an option. Ideally you want to make sure that your features are defined so that your viewers can see you. This will probably mean wearing more and darker makeup than you think looks ideal in real life. "No-makeup-

makeup" isn't the best choice on camera for most. Still, sticking to your innate color parameters (as we discussed in Chapter 4) is of utmost importance, you don't want your viewers spending the entire video looking at your makeup instead of listening to you. You may not normally powder, but shine on your skin can be magnified on camera, so a light dusting will be helpful in keeping your skin lit evenly. While certain shimmer eye shadows can be exquisite for photography or in person, on video they can cause portions of your eyelids to be overly lit and washed out, which can be distracting, so use them with care and when in doubt stick to matte. Always test your makeup just as you would your outfit and be sure that everything checks out. Don't set yourself up for the frustration of loading your footage into your video editor only to find that your foundation looks like the wrong color for your neck on camera and your lipstick bled past your lip lines in the first 5 minutes. Use a magnifying mirror before you press play if you are filming in HD or even more so for 4K. Things you may not be able to notice with your naked eye can turn into a neon flashing sign in modern high resolution videos.

Crafting thoughtful outfits that align with your Signature Style Manifesto is the final step to unlocking your visual potential and leveraging it in your business. Practice this art form and know that the more you do it, the better you will get at it. You may never be the world's greatest stylist, but you absolutely can become a good stylist with a working knowledge of some fantastic tools. Which, as it happens is more than enough to become the master of your own image and the face of your business.

Conclusion

A client who comes to me is usually looking for one thing and one thing only whether she realizes it or not – rules. It seems to be the logical course of action on the surface. The past version of her has, frankly, made a mess of things, and she can't be trusted. Best to find someone who can tell her exactly what to wear and what not to wear in black and white terms down to every last stitch. Ideally, these rules would sound like "Always wear V neck, never wear scoop neck" or "always wear blue red, never wear orange red." The expectation is, of course, that so long as she follows the rules precisely they will always work.

Right? Wrong. Let me be clear, rules have their purpose. But rules alone, no matter how specific, no matter how seemingly foolproof, will not get you what you need. Why? Essentially, because you are intelligent, and rules, no matter how cleverly designed (and yes, that includes by yours truly, or even yourself), are not. If you want to use the rules to rationalize buying a top that doesn't suit you, I promise you will find a way. On the other hand, your intelligence may present you with something utterly perfect for you, but you will pass it up if you follow the rules to the letter (and not because they are inaccurate rules, but simply because crafting an effective image demands a flexibility that no set of rules can encompass). You're even probably smart enough to exaggerate the rules enough to prove the rules don't work.

Rules alone may lead us to worse choices than we made with no rules, because rules essentially shift the burden of decision making outside of oneself. That is, after all, what makes rules so appealing that we are willing to purposefully limit our own freedom. The truth is, there is no way to shift the burden of decision making about your wardrobe and your image and also get the result you desire. Even your own Signature Style Manifesto is not infallible, it simply provides the most likely roadmap to mastering your image. What we need here is a kind of "practical wardrobe wisdom." This "virtue" has two main components, which are as follows:

First, the WILL to master your image and become the face of your business and second, the SKILL to know how to do it.

The will can only come from within you. It's not something I can teach you, give you, or do for you. The good news is that there is no real imperative to have the will to create the right wardrobe. You can simply opt out, and mainly the only person who will be affected is you. The pain of wardrobe frustration and lack of confidence in your appearance may simply not be enough in your life to become greater than the pain of having to take responsibility for changing those things, and that is perfectly legitimate. The decision to stop worrying about it may be the best one you ever made.

It's true that your appearance and how you present yourself will have a major impact on how others perceive you. As sophisticated primates with an enormous visual cortex, that's just how we humans operate. How you look will influence whether people want to work with you, how much they are willing to pay you, what opportunities they will consider offering you, and a million other things that are so subtle it's hard to fathom. Nevertheless, you still have a choice. You get to pick whether you want to strive towards your greatest visual potential or let wherever you are now be enough. I believe that while choices have consequences, there is no way to make the wrong decision here, except perhaps by choosing by default.

So that brings us to number two. Teaching the skill of knowing how to master your image and become the face of your business is what I do. The kind of rules I teach are flexible, and my aim is to teach you the self-awareness to know when and how to bend them, how to improvise, and to do so in the service of the right aims.

The tools in this book are a way of becoming *that* woman. The woman who always looks perfect in her videos each week. The woman whose picture on her website makes you want to buy from her. The woman who knows just what she will wear when Oprah calls. The woman who would never dream of letting her image stand in the way of making the impact she wants to make on the world, because she has faith in her own practical wardrobe wisdom. She may seek help or advice, but at the end of the day the burden of responsibility for her image belongs to her and her alone, as do the accolades for the results.

Like any skill, some will have a natural talent for it, or previous experience that allows them to pick it up more quickly than others. Many women can read this book and find all the answers they need to master their image and create an incredible signature style. Others would benefit from having me there to guide them through the journey. I can be your fashion fairy godmother but only you can be the hero of this story.

Stepping out from behind the curtain and into the spotlight to become the face of your business takes guts. There is always going to be someone who thinks you're too fat or too thin or doesn't like your hair or your nose and who tries to use that as ammunition against you, your work, and your message. It's all just noise unless you let it not be by secretly believing these people are right. When you have accepted your own innate beauty and have elevated it to its highest potential through the vision you created in your Signature Style Manifesto, the words of naysayers can't reach you. The dreaded comments section transforms from a brick wall preventing you from moving forward in your business into a few buzzing gnats that you don't even notice splattering on your windshield as you fly past them at 85 mph, hair flowing in the breeze.

When I guide my clients to make exterior changes using the tools in this book that move them closer to having camera-ready style, they also change their internal vision of themselves. Cinderella doesn't wait to become a princess to wear the dress and the glass slippers, she puts on the dress and the glass slippers and in so doing becomes a princess. Do not wait to take this step until you are ready. Thinking, planning, hoping and dreaming can never make you ready, only doing can do that. The act of mastering your image transforms your perception of yourself from a woman who wants to step up and become the living embodiment of her business and her message to being the woman who already has. Once you've convinced yourself, everything else is easy.

Acknowledgements

I have wanted to write a book for most of my life, but I didn't know I wanted to write this book until a little over 4 years ago when early supporters of my work who I met through Facebook groups and forums about personal style encouraged me to do so. Without the early enthusiasm of my online friends Paisley, Claudia, Kati, Carrie, Lauren and Brooke among many others, as well as that of my "dorm mate" and style partner in crime Claire, my attentions may well have drifted elsewhere far before the first word of this book was written. I am forever grateful for the late night chats about style that got me hooked on the transformational power of this work.

Still, my business would likely never have begun in earnest were it not for Christine Scaman. I went to her to be trained in the art and science of Personal Color Analysis. I was incredibly fortunate to come away not only with a whole new perspective on color and the beauty of nature, but also a confidence in my skills that could only be gained by the acknowledgement of a highly respected teacher, and perhaps best of all, one of the most enriching friendships of my adult life. Thank you for your faith in me from day one, for all you have taught me, for the laughs that have ruined my mascara, and for asking me just how soon I thought I could start taking clients.

To my clients, who have invited me on their journeys, thank you. Watching you step into your own beauty touches my heart and lights the fire within me to keep reaching. An extra special thanks to the Illinois crew and my angelic advocate Athena Butler for always welcoming me with open arms and a bag of snacks, and to Tracy Theemes for your contagious confidence in my work. And to Michelle, Stefanie, June, Erica and Alex who took a leap and tested the path laid out in this book, I am so grateful to you for being willing to boldly go and in so doing help me create a richer experience for many others.

Despite all of that inspiration to write the book from so many amazing people, I can't imagine this book existing without my mentor, Angela Lauria. To thank you for helping me write this book feels like an understatement. Thank you for turning my world upside down and creating a path to what I would have barely dared to dream about.

I could not wrap up this book without acknowledging my husband Steve, my perpetual hype man despite having only a vague notion of what it is I do. Thank you for being there in my dark hours and loving me and believing in me (not to mention always finding a way to make me laugh) all the same.

To the Morgan James Publishing team: Special thanks to David Hancock, CEO & Founder for believing in me and my message. To my Managing Editor, Megan Malone, thanks for making the process seamless and easy. Many more thanks to everyone else, but especially Jim Howard, Bethany Marshall, and Nickcole Watkins.

About the Author

Rachel Nachmias is the founder of Best Dressed Image & Color Consulting. As a graduate of the fashion design program at Parsons the New School for Design, Rachel began her career working behind the scenes of some of New York's top designer labels.

While working as a freelance fashion and costume designer, Rachel discovered life-changing tools that transformed her own personal style and she decided she had to share them with the world. Since then, Rachel has worked her magic on the images and lives of hundreds of clients, turning frustrated ducklings into the beautiful, stylish swans they were always meant to be. She has now shifted her discerning eye to female entrepreneurs, helping them to become camera-ready women of style who know just what to wear when Oprah calls.

Rachel lives in Philadelphia with her husband, her three fluffy toy dogs, and her collection of sparkly chandelier earrings. She enjoys traveling the world, sampling perfume, and curating cheese boards.

Thank You

Thank you for reading *The Face of The Business*. If you've made it this far, I can guess that either you just *really* like me, or (more likely) you're ready to become the face of *your* business. As amazing as that is, insight without action means nothing, so to help you get started, I've created a free toolkit packed with tools to help you start defining your incredible signature style right away. **If you haven't already grabbed it while reading through the book, you can find the toolkit at www. thefaceofthebusiness.com/toolkit.**

I am so excited for you to finally master your image and have the confidence you need to step out on video and let your brilliance shine in your business. I would love to hear how it's going as you work with the tools I've taught you in this book, so feel free to email me at Rachel@bestdressed.us.

Printed in the USA
CPSIA information can be obtained
at www.ICGtesting.com
JSHW012012140824
68134JS00024B/2386